Butterflies

OF BRITAIN AND EUROPE

GREEN GUIDE

Butterflies

OF BRITAIN AND EUROPE

robert and rosemary goodden

ILLUSTRATED BY joyce bee

SELECT EDITIONS

This edition published in 2003 by
Selectabook Ltd.
Roundway, Devizes
Wiltshire SN10 2HT

First published in 1991 by New Holland Publishers (UK) Ltd

1 3 5 7 9 10 8 6 4 2

ISBN 1 84330 507 0

Phototypeset by AKM Associates (UK) Ltd
Reproduction by Scantrans Pte Ltd
Printed and bound in Singapore by
Kyodo Printing Co (Singapore) Pte Ltd

Contents

Introduction

When setting out in search of butterflies for the first time, you should not expect to encounter a myriad of species or large numbers colonising a small area. Butterflies should be looked for in particular types of locality and in regions noted for their Lepidoptera (the scientific order of butterflies and moths).

For instance, a visitor from Britain to the north coast of France will note that the fauna and flora are only a little different from those at home. There are more species to be found but the range becomes greater, and butterflies more numerous, the further south you travel. South of the Loire the potential increases.

There is, however, a sense of anticipation of what is in store. The butterfly enthusiast might be forgiven for hoping to find some excitement round every corner and, indeed, the possibilities of finding the unusual are much greater. A windblown object resembling a leaf just might be an interesting creature, never before encountered. Branches heavily denuded could reveal a colony of some colourful caterpillar that is either rare or does not exist at home. The travelling naturalist will know the feeling well.

Mountainous regions are often well populated, especially in parts of the Alps. Scandinavia has interesting polar species in the extreme north. Centrally there is a gap which is too far north for many of the central European species and too far south for Arctic ones. Clearly, industrialised areas are less productive for butterflies, so it is understandable that sparsely developed parts of central Europe (Czechoslovakia, Poland and south to the Balkans) have wonderful butterfly habitats. Further south, Spain has a very rich butterfly fauna and this is equally true of areas spreading east through southern France, Italy to Greece.

The butterflies on the British List number about 68. In the whole of Europe, there are more than 360 species. Those living in tiny pockets, or at the extremities of the Continent, are not included in this book but, with the exception of some Skippers (Hesperiidae), it has been possible to include most of the butterflies which are likely to be encountered in Europe.

Distribution mentioned in the text for each species refers to mainland regions rather than islands, which tend to have a smaller range of species than nearby mainland. Information on specific island butterfly fauna may be partially available in more comprehensive books but often has to be researched by one's own efforts — work that can be very interesting.

The size given for each species indicates the approximate wingspan.

The symbols and abbreviations which appear on the illustrations denote the following:

♂	male
♀	female
gen 1	1st generation or brood
gen 2	2nd generation or brood
N	northern form
S	southern form
var	variation

The Life Cycle of a Butterfly

Butterflies have a complete metamorphosis, involving four distinct stages in the life cycle. These stages are: egg, larva (caterpillar), pupa (chrysalis) and adult.

The Egg

Eggs may be laid singly, in small groups or in batches, depending on the habits of the individual species. All are visible to the naked eye but they are very small. With a lens, a great deal of interesting detail can be observed and under a low-powered binocular microscope a whole new world of beauty and fascination is opened up. Each species lays eggs that are individual in shape, pattern and colouring. The general characteristics of a family may be observed from the egg, just as this is possible with the adult butterfly itself. The Pierids lay eggs that are tall and bottle-shaped, usually yellow or orange. The Coppers lay eggs that are round, with a very complex and angular construction, deeply pitted and nearly as regular as the pattern of a snowflake.

The duration of the egg stage is dependent on temperature and varies with the species. A typical time would be from two to three weeks and there are hibernating species which remain as eggs from late summer until the following spring.

The outer shell of the egg is rigid, sometimes hard. There is a central closed orifice, the micropyle, through which the egg was fertilised inside the female abdomen, and through which the developing larva is able to breathe. The larval embryo gradually develops by cell division, from almost nothing but a liquid to a fully formed and efficient eating machine. The mandibles are strong and designed to pierce the eggshell once the larva is ready to hatch. A hole is eaten, just large enough to allow the head to break through, and the larva pulls its way out with quite a rapid movement.

The Larva

Larvae grow continuously and may become a thousand times their original size and weight. Their main purpose is to eat and grow. Their skin is elastic but cannot expand enough to accommodate the dramatic increase in size from the newly hatched larva to the final stage, prior to pupation. The problem is solved by changing the skin at intervals, each new one being much larger than the previous one. There are usually at least four skin changes and the periods between changes are known as instars. The first instar lasts until the first skin change and the final stage is the fifth instar, which is followed by pupation. The scientific term for a skin change is *ecdysis*.

As with eggs and the adult butterfly, larve are unique in their colouring, shape and pattern, though there are often great similarities between species in any genus. Some larvae are solitary, others live gregariously.

A larva makes a very nourishing snack for a bird or other predator and it is in the larval stage that the greatest losses take place. Larvae are therefore often well camouflaged to blend with the particular foodplant or location they normally inhabit. Frequently they lie hidden by day and only stir to feed under the cover of darkness. Gregarious larvae are usually not camouflaged and are often dark coloured or black, thus presenting a formidable mass that is off-putting to a predator. A few are strikingly coloured and very prominent: these are usually poisonous and use warning colours to advertise the fact.

The larval stage usually lasts from one to two months but, as with the other stages, this is dependent on temperature and species.

There are many larvae which hibernate; thus their life can be nine or ten months.

The Pupa

The change from active larva to totally static and quite differently shaped pupa is one of nature's greatest wonders. At the end of the final instar (the fifth instar in the case of most species) there is one more skin change. The skin splits on the thorax, just behind the head; the head capsule is finally cast off, and the skin is wriggled back to the tail end and finally shed. The appearance of the creature is still rather like the hunched-up larva before the change, but it is glistening wet and has some features of the pupa. As the pre-pupa dries, the pupal characters become more pronounced and the colour often changes. The drying and formation of the pupa may take a few hours, or even up to a day.

Before this final event, the larva must seek a suitable place in which to pupate. Butterfly larvae almost never spin a cocoon and so need to find a concealed spot where the immobile pupa will be safe from predation.

There are three terms which describe the way in which a pupa is situated or suspended.

Suspensi describes those pupae that are attached simply by the tail, hanging free, with head downwards. All Satyridae and Nymphalidae pupae are suspensi. So too are other closely related families. The extreme tail tip, known as the *cremaster*, carries tiny but dense hooks which give a firm grip on the silk pad that the larva has spun as an anchorage. This situation poses an interesting problem for the larva which has the task of casting its final skin. If it lets go its firm hold on the silk pad, to shrug off the old larval skin, there is nothing to stop it from plunging to the ground. In fact it does not fall; the pre-pupa unhooks itself, flicks away the skin and re-attaches itself in the blink of an eye, all with total success.

Succincti is a twofold method of attachment – belt and braces. The attachment is also at the tail, but the pupa is not hanging head downwards. The larva spins a girdle of silk around the junction of the thorax and abdomen. This sling holds the pupa with head upwards, against a stem, which may be vertical or angled upwards. The same quick movement is necessary to slough off the old larval skin, but the support of the girdle makes the operation less hazardous. The Pieridae and Lycaenidae pupae are succincti.

Involuti pupae are those that are lying loose, or enveloped in silk. Butterfly pupae do not have true cocoons in the sense of moth cocoons, but the Graylings pupate loose at the foot of grass tussocks and some of the Skippers make a loose tent of grass blades and silk, in which the pupa is formed.

Inside the newly formed pupal case, the process is not dissimilar to the activity inside the egg. At first the main contents comprise essential organs immersed in blood. There are the minute beginnings of the features of the adult, but these exist as small groups of cells known as *imaginal buds*. The cells subdivide and grow into the recognisable features of the adult, such as the legs, proboscis, eyes and, of course, the wings. A look at the exterior of the pupal case shows the outward form of these same features.

The Adult

The adult can be seen forming inside the pupal case in the last days before it is ready to emerge. The last signs are the bright colours which show through the wing cases. When it is ready to emerge, the adult breaks open the pupal case, pulls itself out and seeks a place where it can hang and expand its wings. The growth of the wings is almost fast enough to observe and the full length is achieved in something like twenty minutes. The wings are very soft and floppy for about an hour and the butterfly is vulnerable at this stage if found by a predator. Once the wings are dry the butterfly is ready to fly and it begins its life in search of nectar and a mate. The life of the adult may be as short as a few days, just enough time to breed; but in the case of some species the adult may live for weeks and even months. Some temperate species hibernate as adults, not breeding until the spring, and will have a life of perhaps ten months.

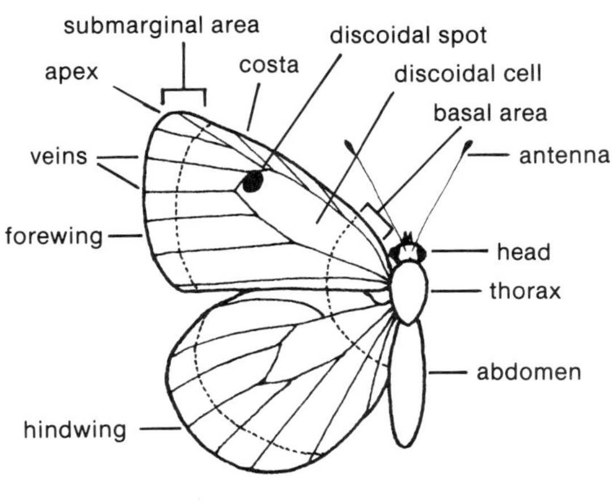

Scent Brands

Scent brands (also known as sex brands) occur only on male butterflies. They are marks or patches of scent-scales (*androconia*) which contain pheremones, essential to courtship. Not all butterflies have scent brands but they are important to those that do possess them. The following are some examples:

Hairstreaks
Certain Hairstreaks (e.g. Green and White Letter) have a small oval scent-scale patch close to the leading edge of the forewing.

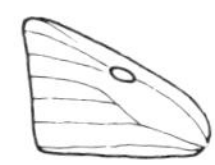

Browns
Scent-scales cover quite large areas of the forewing in most of the Satyridae. In the case of the Walls, Gatekeeper and Speckled Wood, they form part of the patterning and may not seem obvious. On the *Erebias* the dark patch on dark ground colour may conceal the *androconia*, but the silky texture and slight greenish, iridescent hue in some lights, reveal the dense scent-scale area.

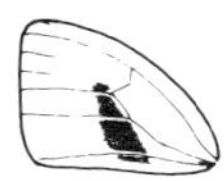

Silver-washed Fritillary
Parallel rows of scent brands are situated along the central veins of the forewing.

Skippers
In some of the Hesperiidae the scent brand is particularly prominent as a strong, oblique slashmark that is sometimes instrumental in distinguishing the species.

Milkweeds
Milkweeds have a raised (three dimensional), pocket-like patch on the hindwing.

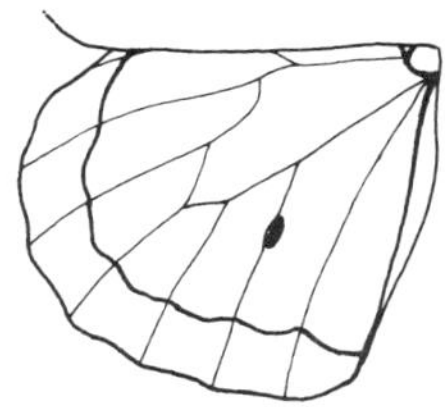

Butterfly Habitats

Dense woodland does not suit butterflies but woodland localities with open rides, clearings and wild surrounds provide wonderful hunting ground. Here may be found the delicate Hairstreaks, sometimes the powerful Nymphalids such as the White Admiral, possibly Purple Emperor, Fritillaries, Large Tortoiseshell, Camberwell Beauty, the Peacock and Comma. Brimstones like woodland also. If uncultivated grassland surrounds the woodland, then the range will include many more species which mingle with the woodland butterflies.

Wild meadows and grazed downland often support a wide variety of butterflies. These include especially the Blues, Coppers, Skippers and the Satyrids. Some of the Vanessids (Peacock and Tortoiseshell family) will also be found in these grassy areas.

Wetlands have a few specialised butterflies (notably the Coppers) but such damp areas are seldom noted for a great abundance or variety of species. However, the fens are sometimes a stronghold for many moths that depend on their specialised reeds and rushes as foodplants.

In high summer, on hot days, mud puddles and edges of streams often attract butterflies, especially in the mountains. It is not only the moisture that they seek but the salts rising up from the soil.

Heaths and moorlands often have their own characteristic and interesting butterflies. These are not as varied and numerous as grassland species but well worth studying.

Gardens, well stocked with flowers, provide wonderful opportunities for watching butterflies. Here will be the stronghold of the Vanessids, Whites, Brimstones, Orange Tips and Clouded Yellows, and even Swallowtails. The Holly Blue frequently breeds in gardens. If there are nearby woods or grassland, even more butterflies will visit the garden for nectar.

Some of the finest habitat for butterflies is to be found in mountains. There is great diversity according to the vegetation and altitude. The giant Apollo butterfly is one of the most spectacular. There are Fritillaries, not only many species but also some specialised high altitude ones that often dance about in the snow, way above the level of any vegetation. High up also there are the Polar Graylings (*Oenis*) and some specialised Clouded Yellows. Blues, Coppers, Skippers and Browns exist often in astonishing variety and number. In mountain regions, a field of lucerne or lavender in flower can have such butterflies as you might only dream of, if you are used to more northern places. Species such as the Large Blue, Scarce Swallowtail, Queen of Spain Fritillary and Large Copper may all be seen together, and in great numbers.

Studying and Breeding Butterflies

For many, it is enough enjoyment simply to be out in the countryside amongst flowery fields and butterflies. Others may wish to have more purpose and gradually build up a photographic collection. Some enthusiasts still make collections of butterflies but this can be harmful to localised and endangered populations and is now considered rather unnecessary, except for specific scientific work.

Breeding butterflies can bring a great deal of pleasure and greatly add to your knowledge. Much goes on in the early stages that is unobserved in the field. Only by breeding was Berger's Clouded Yellow discovered, as recently as 1947. The adult is so similar to the Pale Clouded Yellow that the difference was only recognised when the larvae were produced in captivity: those of Berger's are heavily marked with black and yellow on green whilst Pale Clouded Yellow larvae are plain green with minimal markings. Whilst studying the early stages of butterflies may not reveal spectacular discoveries of this nature very often, you can learn much about a species and gain great satisfaction from raising butterflies from larvae.

Butterfly larvae may be found or bought. It is not advantageous to take a mass of larvae from the wild; collect just enough of a gregarious species (say, 20) to maintain their gregarious habit but leave the rest remaining wild. One of the best species to start breeding is the Small Tortoiseshell (*Aglais urticae*). It is quite common and lives in colonies, so it is not harmful to take a few. The total life of the larva is about a month, so wild-collected ones may pupate in as little as a fortnight and, with a pupal period of barely two weeks, the butterflies emerge often in less than a month from the start of rearing. It is much more specialised to get the butterflies to pair and lay eggs in captivity, and the beginner is advised to release the butterflies either where found as larvae, or into suitable habitat.

It should be stressed that many larvae found in the wild will be those of moths and they are equally interesting to rear. As a rule, use the foodplant on which they are found. If this fails, experiment with various plants but return the larva to where it was found if it does not feed in the first day. Larva identification can be difficult and few books are comprehensive enough to help.

If you choose to rear on potted foodplants, enclose the plant in netting to prevent escape. The food stays fresh and conditions are hygenic, but change the plant before it is half eaten: it can be harmful to make the larvae finish all the plant. A few butterfly larvae pupate at the foot of the plant, but most will attach themselves either to the netting or the foodplant. Leave the pupa in place to hatch; though if it is an overwintering pupa it is often better to remove it carefully and store it loose in a plastic box in a cool outhouse or fridge.

Another method of rearing is in clear, transparent plastic boxes, on cut foodplants. Close attention and daily care is needed, otherwise disease can develop. Line the box with slightly absorbent paper. Use a fine paintbrush to move the larvae, very gently. Fine-pointed forceps are useful for cleaning out the box. Each day, remove the paper lining and contents. Put in a fresh lining and then the parts of foodplant that have larvae on, having first cut away old food that has no larvae attached. Put the new foodplant (never wet) *on top* of the larvae, and close the lid. The box contains sufficient air and should not be perforated in order to maintain the freshness of the foodplant. *Plastic boxes must not be stood in the sun* as this produces intense heat and humidity and will quickly kill the larvae.

It is usually best to transfer larger larvae to a cage some time before pupation, partly beause they need more space and food, but also because the box is rather too humid an environment for pupation. Larvae escape easily, so doors need to be close fitting. The best design of cage is one with a wooden frame, covered with nylon netting. Diseases occur commonly in larvae. Causes can be crowding, poor quality or shortage of foodplant, excessive humidity (as in a plastic box) and simply forgetting to clean out and change the contents each day. Parasitic flies can be a problem if the cage netting is not fine enough but the risk is greater when rearing out of doors rather than inside.

A wood-framed netting cage is also suitable for breeding butterflies. The dimensions depend on the size and quantity of butterflies, and the size and type of foodplant; about 40 cubic centimetres might be suitable but the exact measurements are not critical. Butterflies require fresh foodplants (usually potted), flowers for nectar, and sufficient sunlight to keep them active. Arrange the foodplant within about 5 centimetres from the top of the cage; also keep the nectar flowers high up where the butterflies will find them. Some butterflies lay eggs singly, others in batches. Technique is improved with experience and the choice of species for a beginner is important.

When breeding butterflies, find out whether they will produce another brood that year, or whether they will overwinter. Only a few species hibernate as pupae (the most convenient stage). Some remain as eggs which are also comparatively easy to keep. Those that hibernate as adults are really quite difficult and it is better to free them than to let them die. The majority pass the winter as larvae and they do best kept out of doors even in extreme weather conditions. They are subject to predation, and hibernation is often unsuccessful, so think carefully before embarking on hibernating larvae. Pupae and eggs are best stored in tightly fitting plastic boxes in a very cool outhouse or refrigerator.

Codes for Collecting and Breeding Butterflies

The following points are extracted from the *Code for Insect Collecting* published by the Joint Committee for the Conservation of British Insects:

Do not kill an insect just in order to examine or identify it. Carry collecting boxes for easy inspection. Release again in the same place as caught.

Introduction

Do not collect all that can be found; take only one or a few.

For commercial purposes, insects should either be bred or obtained from old collections.

Endangered species should be left undisturbed.

Always seek permission from the landowner before entering land.

Do not damage crops or wild habitat. Tracks through hayfields may spoil the crop. Do not trample wild flowers or cut ways through hedgerows. Cut the foodplant cleanly — do not break the stem.

Extracts from the Code for Butterfly Establishment, published by the British Butterfly Conservation Society

Some definitions:
Introduction: An attempt to establish a species where it was not previously known. **Reintroduction:** A further attempt.

Re-establishment: An attempt to found a colony where a natural population has died out.

Support breeding or **Population reinforcement:** An attempt to increase population size by releasing additional individuals.

Translocation: Transfer of individuals from a threatened site.

Efforts should be directed towards re-establishment where natural populations have died out since 1900.

The BBCS believes that priority should be given to re-establishing species that stand a reasonable chance of spreading to form additional colonies, rather than species that live in small and wholly isolated sites.

People wishing to attempt reintroduction, or any of the above categories, are encouraged to inform and consult with the British Butterfly Conservation Society and the local Trust for Nature Conservation.

It is considered undesirable to release non-indigenous species into the wild and it also contravenes the Wildlife and the Countryside Act.

Conservation

Conservation is now a vital issue, one to which we can all contribute and one that affects every person in the world, not just naturalists and ecologists.

The following are some ways in which we can be of direct help, both individually and by joining in with others. (Addresses of useful organisations will be found on page 99.)

If you own a garden you can grow plants to feed and attract butterflies. It is a pleasure to watch them and the butterflies benefit from having a source of nectar to build them up before hibernation. As well as flowerbeds, preserve a few wild patches of rough ground where bramble, grass, thistles and nettles can all play their part and may help to establish or reinforce wild colonies.

Land management for butterflies is becoming important. Many species thrive where the habitat is kept in a suitable condition for them, but decline if the habitat is left to become overgrown. If you do not own land, you may find places where a landowner will let you manage the habitat for butterflies. You can obtain advice from your county Trust for Nature or the British Butterfly Conservation Society.

Help to interest children in conservation — your own family, schools, youth organisations. Introduce them to butterfly charts, books and conservation societies. Show them that the ecology of the environment is important and that plant life and habitats need to be conserved as well as butterflies themselves. Give to a young person a year's membership of the British Butterfly Conservation Society.

Help to organise local displays, activities, talks and slide shows. Try to interest the local press in reports and articles about butterflies and conservation.

Notice disturbance of wild places and confer with conservation organisations if a habitat appears to be in danger.

Join the British Butterfly Conservation Society and your local county Nature Conservation Trust. This enables you to keep in touch with current conservation activities through their journals. You can take part in practical habitat management schemes and both meet and correspond with others who are active and interested in conservation.

Support conservation efforts with a donation of money. Help conservation organisations with fund-raising and to obtain sponsorship from industry and charitable trusts. The management and purchase of reserves is beginning to have a beneficial effect on butterfly populations and may become vital for the future survival of some species.

Families of Butterflies

Papilionidae (Swallowtails)
Swallowtails include the largest butterflies in the world. In Europe there are four large black and yellow tailed species, though not all Papilios have tails. This family also has in Europe three species of mountain Apollos (*Parnassius*), and three curious Festoons which have characteristics in common with both the Apollos and the Swallowtails. The larvae of Papilionidae possess a forked organ (the *osmeterium*) behind the head which is ejected and emits a pungent smell if the larva is disturbed. Festoon larvae feed on birthworts (*Aristolochia*) and they have colours that warn of the poisons they contain from the foodplant. Papilio larvae are attached to a stem by the tail and a silken girdle round the thorax (*succincti*).

Pieridae (Whites and Sulphurs)
A family of about 40 European species which have predominantly white, yellow and orange colouring, with black markings, sometimes tinged with green. The apparent green markings on the underside of Orange Tips and some of the Bath White group are in fact a curious mixture of black and yellow scales. Some of the *Colias* have true pale green colouring; others are edged with a beautiful pale pink, which is also seen on the antennae and sometimes the legs. The Pieridae include the garden Whites, Brimstones, Orange Tips and Clouded Yellows; their coloration is usually derived from pigments in the larval foodplants. Many Pierids feed on the cabbages and cresses (Cruciferae), other groups, notably the Clouded Yellows, feed on trefoils and other Papilionaceae. The larvae have a characteristic shape, being long and slender with blunt tapering at either end; many have a decorated lateral line. The pupae are always fixed by the tail (*cremaster*) and with a girdle round the abdomen (*succincti*).

Danaidae
In Europe two species have settled and become established in the Azores and Canary Isles — the Milkweed and its smaller relative, the Plain Tiger. Both feed on milkweeds (*Asclepias spp*) which are not hardy and grow in only the warmest parts of Europe. All stages in the life history contain poisons derived from the foodplant, and their colouring, both as adults and as larvae, warns predators of the poison. Other, palatable, species mimic the Danaids and thus escape predation. In winter the life cycle continues but at a slow rate. The Milkweed is known in America as the Monarch and in Australia as the Wanderer. It is famous for its ability to travel thousands of miles by migration. Rare examples are found in Britain after travelling all the way across the Atlantic Ocean.

Libytheidae
Europe has just one species (the Nettle Tree Butterfly) in this genus of snout butterflies, which is so named because of the pronounced palpi which form a nose. Species are found on most of the continents of the world but, as in Europe, usually only one, or very few different species, are seen in any particular region.

Nymphalidae
This is one of the most important of all butterfly families. It includes the garden Vanessids, such as the Peacock and Red Admiral, the Fritillaries, the Purple Emperor and White Admiral. In tropical countries many of the robust and colourful butterflies are Nymphalids. The particular characteristic of this family is that the

forelegs are degenerate. The butterfly appears to have only four legs; there are six but the front pair are smaller, clawless and held tight to the thorax, not used for walking. The forelegs have rows of strong bristles, hence the name given to the Nymphalidae — the brush-footed butterflies.

Satyridae (Browns)
The overall colour of this family is brown or yellowish-orange, with the exception of the Marbled Whites which rather more resemble the Pieridae. The chief groups in this family are the Meadow Browns, Graylings, Ringlets, Heaths, Marbled Whites, Speckled Woods and Walls, and the Arctic Graylings (*Oenis*). Nearly a third of European butterflies are in this family. The most important characteristic is the thickening of the forewing veins into nodes at the junction with the thorax. This is seen in all species. Satyrid larvae are all grass-feeders; they have a typical shape that tapers sharply towards the tail and rather less so towards the head. Most are striped from head to tail, giving camouflage amongst grasses. While most are coloured in shades of green, those found amongst dried grasses are in matching shades of buff and ochre. The pupae are usually suspended from the tail (*suspensi*) but some Graylings are formed lying loosely (*involuti*) on the ground at the base of the foodplant.

Nemeobiidae (Metalmarks)
In Europe the sole member of this family is the Duke of Burgundy Fritillary. The butterfly has markings like the Fritillaries (Nymphalidae) but the Nemeobiidae have six walking legs and smaller characters which differentiate the two. Most Metalmarks occur in South America where the family is represented by numerous, often highly colourful and iridescent species. There are many likenesses to the Lycaenidae. This is also seen in the woodlouse-shaped larvae and hunched, rounded pupae that are girdle fixed (*succincti*).

Lycaenidae (Blues, Coppers and Hairstreaks)
All species are relatively small; the smallest butterflies in the world are Lycaenids. This family comprises about a quarter of Europe's butterflies. Larvae of Lycaenids are short and dumpy, tapering bluntly at either end, in the form of a woodlouse. Many of the larvae have strong associations with ants which tend them, cleaning them and drinking honeydew secretion from a gland (unique to Lycaenid larvae) near the tail. The larvae undoubtedly derive benefit from the ants and possibly escape much predation as a result. The genus *Maculinea* (Large Blues) actually live their larval life inside ants' nests

where they feed, not on plants, but on the ant brood. The pupa is formed within the ants' nest; from here the butterfly emerges and escapes through an ant tunnel to the outside world where it expands and dries its wings, ready to fly free.

There are three distinct groups of butterflies in this family:

The Blues: Some of these are brown in both sexes or in the female only. They are characterised by their undersides with rows of small, usually pupilled spots. The majority are found in grassland and commonly feed on trefoils, though some have rather more specialised foodplant requirements.

The Coppers: Mostly a fiery, true burnished copper colour; some are heavily spotted, a few are mostly dark brown and some are suffused with iridescent purple. Coppers feed on sorrels, docks and polygonums.

The Hairstreaks: Characterised by underside zig-zag markings, and usually with short delicate tails. The larvae usually feed on trees and shrubs, boring into the buds of both leaves and flowers and living concealed inside for much of their lives.

Hesperiidae (Skippers)
This family is thought to be primitive and ancient in terms of evolution. There are characters of both butterflies and moths and some authors in the past have separated the Skippers into a sub-order of their own. The eyes are widely separated, and there is a bristle at the base of each antenna, like an eyelash; this is not found in other Lepidoptera. The body is thick and robust. The orange-chestnut Skippers (Hesperiinae) have a curious resting position, with the hindwings held not quite horizontal and forewings held higher and at an angle. The numerous Grizzled Skippers (Pyriginae) rest with their wings outspread and the Dingy Skipper chooses between the same resting position and holding its wings tent-like over its body like a moth. Skipper larvae live in a shelter constructed with silk amongst the foodplant; they are never seen feeding loose and they even pupate in the shelter. They are able to catapult their droppings some distance, so as not to leave a tell-tale pile to give away their hiding place.

Papilionids

Swallowtail *Papilio machaon* 80–90mm. Inhabits open country and waysides up to higher altitudes. In Britain (ssp *britannicus*) found only in Norfolk Broads where it is scarce and protected. Several subspecies distributed throughout Europe. Common, especially central and southern Europe. Two broods are usual, flying May–September, but in warmer southern areas there may be more broods and a longer flight period. Larva colourful, green, striped and marked with black and orange, with concealed defensive aromatic organ (*osmeterium*) that is projected if disturbed; most commonly found on fennel (milk parsley in Norfolk). Pupa overwinters.

Scarce Swallowtail *Iphiclides podalirius* 80mm. Flies at woodland edges and in open country, in central and southern Europe; absent from Britain. Common in southern regions. Not easily bred. An avid nectar feeder and very partial to lavender flowers; often visits gardens. A subspecies, *feisthemali*, from southern France and Spain, is white with contrasting dark pattern and deeper blue hindwing spots. Two broods; flight season April/May–September. Larva is peculiarly shaped and patterned to be concealed on the leaves of blackthorn; it is also found on other *Prunus* species and sometimes on hawthorn. Pupa overwinters.

Festoon *Zerynthia polyxena* 50–60mm. Flies in open country. Found across southern Europe to Greece and beyond; absent from Spain. Local; range limited by the presence of foodplant, birthwort, which naturally occurs in scrub and particularly amongst cultivated vineyards. The Festoon belongs to the Swallowtails (Papilionidae), small for this family, and with some of the characteristics of the Apollos. The larva is curiously fat, with red to red-brown, black-tufted tubercles; often found in small groups. Pupa overwinters.

Apollo *Parnassius apollo* 80–90mm. Very grand mountain species, found in Alpine meadows, on slopes and in valleys. Range includes Scandinavia, Spain, the Alps, and eastwards to Greece. Protected in some countries where it is becoming scarcer, though common in certain regions. Male distinctly snow white, with contrasting markings in red and black. Female translucent, wings rather more rounded. Confusion possible with the smaller *P. phoebus*. Single brood; flight season July–September. The winter is passed in the egg stage. The very prominent larva feeds on species of stonecrop.

♂

♀

♂

♀

Large White *Pieris brassicae* 60mm. Universally encountered in fields, waysides, woodland and gardens. Female distinguished by extra forewing spotting. Seasonal colour variation; the spring underside is peppery or speckled; summer underside colouring is a clearer white. Two or more broods; often breeds harmlessly on wasteland, feeding on wild Cruciferae including horseradish, cresses, wild brassicas and honesty. Flight season April–October. Gregarious larvae often encountered on nasturtium; prone to attack by small parasitic wasps (*Apanteles glomeratus*) found as clusters of tiny yellow cocoons on the dead larva. Winter pupa.

Small White *Pieris rapae* 50mm. Probably Europe's widest spread and commonest butterfly, found in all regions. Female has more forewing spotting than male. Differs from Large White in size and markings which are softer and paler. Dependent on region, there may be two to four broods in the year. Flight season April–October in most of Europe but may be February–December in hot countries. Larva lives singly, on cabbage and other Cruciferae, often burrowing through tightly packed leaves and becoming concealed. Winter pupa.

Green-veined White *Pieris napi* 50mm. Not one of the 'Cabbage Whites', this is a woodland and wayside butterfly which strays into gardens but does not cause damage. Common throughout Europe and subject to much seasonal and geographical variation. Irish and Scottish races often have very bright yellow colouring. In colder parts and at higher altitudes, the veining becomes very dark and thick; the high alpine ssp *bryoniae* is almost totally suffused with brown scaling and thick veins. At least two broods; flies April–October. Larva lives singly on Cruciferae, usually cresses, garlic mustard and horseradish. Pupa overwinters.

Bath White *Pontia daplidice* 50mm. Strong migrant, found in open fields and waysides, on beaches and in gardens. Very rare visitor to Britain and northern Europe; common in southern Europe. Several similar species but most are rare and local. Female more heavily marked than male. Continuously brooded. The larva feeds on mignonette, *Arabis* and *Sinapis*. This butterfly being Mediterranean in origin, its winter stage may be larval or pupal but is never quite dormant.

Peak White *Pontia callidice* 35mm. A high altitude butterfly occurring on grassy slopes and high crags at about 2,000m and more. Found in the Pyrenees and Alps. Very local and uncommon. Colour similar to the Bath White but the dense pattern of white or pale yellow chevrons on the underside hindwing distinguishes it from other species. There is one brood. Flight season is in May and June. The larva feeds on mignonette and mustards. Winter pupa.

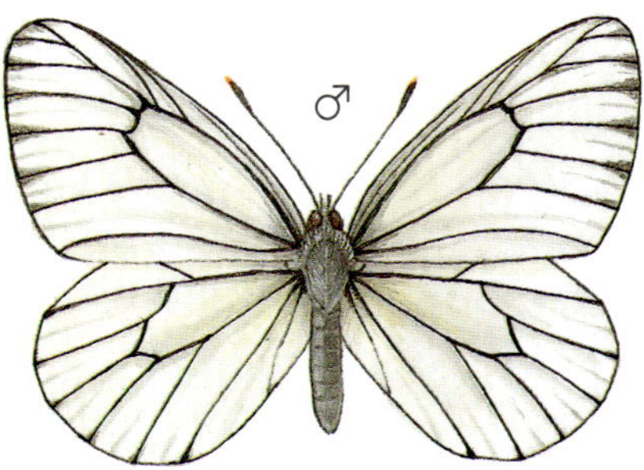

Black-veined White *Aporia crataegi* 60mm. Found at woodland edges and along hedgerows. Mostly common in Europe, in places up to some considerable altitude; extinct in Britain since about 1911. Female rather transparent due to sparse scaling. Flies from late June to August. Sometimes seen clustering at wet mud patches, in company with Skippers and Blues. The larva feeds on bushes of blackthorn and hawthorn, forming a web in which it hibernates concealed amongst silk and dead leaves. Pupa attractively coloured in yellow, white and black: warning colours shunned by predators.

Orange Tip *Anthocharis cardamines* 40mm. One of the first signs of spring, seen along lanes and hedgerows, edges of woodland and even in gardens. Common throughout Europe. Female difficult to distinguish from the Whites in flight but the orange tips of the male catch the eye. Underside has green mottled markings giving camouflage on flowerheads of foodplant, garlic mustard. Single brood; flies April–June (July in mountains). Eggs may be laid on cuckoo flower and other Cruciferae. Larva cannibalistic when young; slender and green, shaded with highlight that gives wonderful camouflage. Thorn-like winter pupa is equally camouflaged.

Mountain Clouded Yellow *Colias phicomone* 50mm. Not uncommon, though local, at altitudes of 1,800m or more, in the Pyrenees and Alps. In sunshine, quite a number may be visible at a time, visiting nectar-bearing rock plants. The moment the sun goes in, the butterflies disappear. Male is characteristically greenish-grey; female upperside is a bright off-white ground colour. Both sexes are fringed with delightful pink. Single brooded; flight season June–August. Small larva overwinters, often covered by snow, concealed at the base of the foodplants, which are horseshoe vetch and allied vetches.

Moorland Clouded Yellow *Colias palaeno* 50mm. A butterfly of heathland and bog, found rather locally in northern European and Scandinavian countries. The species occurs southwards to central eastern France and Switzerland; not found in Britain. Becoming scarcer and protected in some regions. The male is a most unusual lime green; female distinguished by lighter, almost white, colouring. There are three distinct geographical races, not easily distinguished in appearance but defined by locality. Single brood; flight period is in June and July. The larva hibernates on its foodplant, blueberry.

Clouded Yellow *Colias crocea* 50mm. Found particularly in fields of clover and lucerne and on cliff-tops. Originates from North Africa and the Mediterranean, spreading northwards from spring until late summer. In certain years large numbers reach Britain and northern Europe. Female distinguished by spotting in the black wing border; a small proportion of females (var. *helice*) have a white or cream background. Continuously brooded. Normal flight season May–October but in the Mediterranean may be seen in February. In winter, survives only in extreme south. The larva feeds on clover, lucerne and vetches.

Pale Clouded Yellow *Colias hyale* 50mm. Found particularly in fields of lucerne and in open country. Very rare migrant in Britain and northern Europe, but in the south this butterfly is commoner than the Clouded Yellow. Male ground colour is lemon yellow, that of the female is nearer white. There is a similar species, Berger's Clouded Yellow, from which it is almost indistinguishable. Multi-brooded, flying from May–October. Winter larva, growing slowly on clover, lucerne and other Papilionaceae.

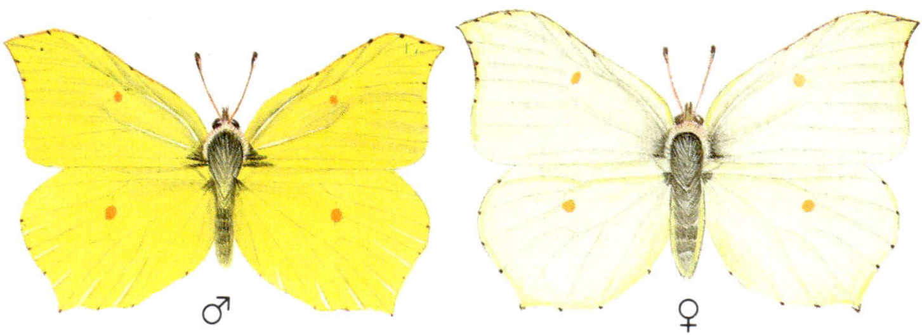

Brimstone *Gonepteryx rhamni* 60mm. Favours woodland clearings but also seen in open country, fields and gardens. Common throughout Europe. Male bright yellow; female pale green, almost white; in resting position resembles shape and colour of ivy leaves, which is where it hibernates. Single brood. Seen as early as February, but most numerous in July. Larva feeds on alder buckthorn, which is found primarily as a woodland shrub, and purging buckthorn, which favours chalk downland. The butterflies are encountered individually, often in places where the foodplant is totally absent.

Cleopatra's Brimstone *Gonepteryx cleopatra* 60mm. A beautiful south European Brimstone, seen in flowery meadows, woodland, fields of clover and lavender, and often in mountains. Restricted to the extreme south of France and regions southwards. Locally common. Male forewings are flushed with bright orange. The butterflies pass the winter as adults, in partial hibernation. The larva feeds on buckthorn, though there is a possibility that it may live on other plants as buckthorn is not in evidence in many places where the butterflies are plentiful.

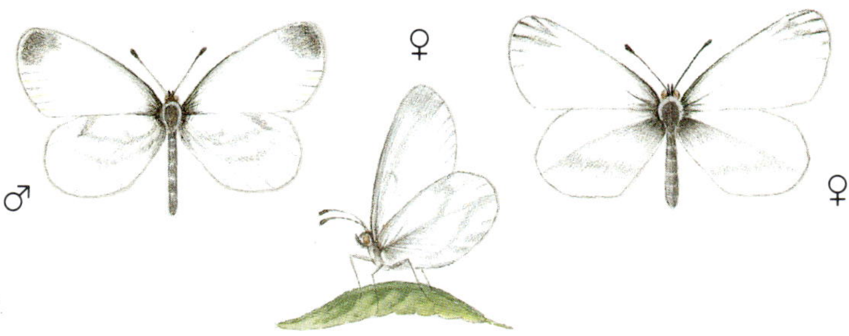

Wood White *Leptidea sinapis* 40mm. Essentially a woodland butterfly, but found also in adjoining meadows. In Britain local or uncommon; elsewhere in Europe widespread and locally common. The slow, floppy flight distinguishes the Wood White from the other Whites. Male has rather darker charcoal tips to the wings but both sexes are very variable in the depth of colouring on both the underside and upperside. There are two broods; flight season May–August. The larva feeds on tufted and allied vetches. Winter is passed in the pupal stage; a slender, green chrysalis that is attached to a twig.

Milkweed Butterfly *Danaus plexippus* 100mm. World famous as the strongest migrant, the Milkweed has established itself in parts of the Canary Isles and Madeira. Originating in North America, adults migrate, rarely, across the Atlantic to the shores of Britain. Male is distinguished by a small black pouch of scent scales on a vein of the hindwing. All stages in the life history are highly poisonous, due to toxins in the normal larval foodplant, milkweed. The larva is strikingly coloured in yellow and black, usually a deterrent to predators.

Nettle Tree Butterfly *Libythea celtis* 40mm. A migrant species that is not often encountered. There is no particular type of terrain that this butterfly favours. The sole foodplant is the nettle tree, which grows only in the southern countries of Europe. This restricts the distribution, which occurs throughout Spain, along the south of France, Italy and eastwards through Yugoslavia to Greece. Remarkably camouflaged while at rest, whether resting on bark or amongst leaves. It is in this stage that it hibernates in early autumn. There is just one brood.

Nymphalids

Two-tailed Pasha *Charaxes jasius* 75–80mm. A magnificent and powerful butterfly, the only European species in its genus which has its stronghold in Africa. Lives along the south coasts of Spain, France, Italy and westwards to Greece. Attracted to tree sap, fruit and even carrion, and can sometimes be lured by bait; seldom a nectar-feeder. There are two broods, in May–June and in August–September. The larva is very exotic; the head has a 'crown of thorns', the shape is rather fat and oval which gives the larva concealment on the oval leaves of its foodplant, the strawberry tree.

Purple Emperor *Apatura iris* 60–65mm. Flies high in woodland; its main habitats are ancient oak woods. Occurs in northern and central Europe (including southern England) except Scandinavia. Rare in Britain, local elsewhere. Sexes differ, the male having a purple iridescent shading on the upperside which is usually visible only on one pair of wings at a time. Adults feed from liquids such as sap, honeydew, dung and carrion. Single brood, flying July–August. Eggs laid singly. Larva solitary; over-winters, turning a bark colour in autumn and back to green in spring, both stages providing excellent camouflage; foodplant sallow.

Lesser Purple Emperor
Apatura ilia 55–60mm. Flies in woodlands in central and southern Europe, excluding Britain. Also found flying low along valleys. Similar to the Purple Emperor, though smaller and tends to be more marked with grey and black. Has one or sometimes two broods, seen in May and June initially, and often in August and September. Larva small, solitary; hibernates on a twig, turning from a bark colour in autumn to green in spring. Foodplants are willows and poplars, especially *P. tremula* and *P. nigra*.

♂ ♀

♂

Poplar Admiral *Limenitis populi* 80mm. This species is scarce, but can be found flying in light woodland and alongside rivers in parts of central and northern Europe, excluding Britain. Large butterfly with some resemblance to a female Purple Emperor though distinguished by an orange submarginal band. Single brood, flying June–July. The larva spends the winter in an individual hibernaculum; feeds mainly on aspen but sometimes accepts other poplars. The pupa, often concealed in a furled leaf, is very knobbly, a typical feature of the *Limenitis* genus.

♂

♂

Southern White Admiral *Limenitis reducta* 50mm. Flies at woodland edges. Occurs in central and southern Europe, but not Britain. Not rare. Can be confused with the White Admiral though white markings are broader and the background usually blacker; wings more rounded; underside brick red rather than orange. Two or three broods occur in southern Europe, but only one in northern Switzerland. Flies May–July. Eggs laid singly on upper leaf surfaces. Larva hibernates; is an attractive pale green with brown spines; foodplant honeysuckle. The pupa is grey with silvery markings, and hangs from a twig, camouflaged like a leaf.

White Admiral *Limenitis camilla* 50mm. Flies in large woods in central Europe, including southern England; loves bramble blossom. Female has slightly more rounded wings and is not quite so black as the male. Single brood. Flight season June–August. Eggs laid singly on the edge of leaves of the foodplant, honeysuckle. The larva is spiny brown in autumn, and pale green in spring, having hibernated in an intricate hibernaculum made with a folded leaf; the young larva conceals itself with particles of its droppings mixed with silk in the form of a tube, positioning itself at the leaf tip.

Hungarian Glider *Neptis rivularis* 60mm. Flies in open woodland in Austria and central east Europe. Not rare where it occurs, but its localities are restricted. Its flight is particularly charming, with little flits and then long glides that characterise this genus. Though patterned rather like the White Admiral, its narrow wings and smaller size separate the two. The sexes are similar. There are two broods; the butterflies are seen in May/June, and then into July and September. The larva constructs a hibernaculum on its foodplant, *Spiraea*.

Camberwell Beauty *Nymphalis antiopa* 80mm. Very rare migrant to Britain where it was first found in Camberwell, London. Widely distributed in Europe, flying in open woods and scrubland, from June–August and, after hibernation, from March–April. In Europe and America, known as the Mourning Cloak, referring to the pale frill on the wing margins like a dress beneath a dark cloak. Eggs laid in spring, in clusters round a twig. Larvae gregarious; attractively coloured in black and red with spines; spin a fresh communal web after each moult; foodplants willow, sallow, birch and elm.

Nymphalids

Large Tortoiseshell *Nymphalis polychloros* 80mm. Flies at woodland edges, in fields and hedgerows. Widely distributed in Europe, though very rare in Britain. There is one brood; the butterflies emerge in late June or July and go into early hibernation without feeding. They come out of hibernation in April to bask in the sun, and are more attracted to liquids than flowers. The eggs are laid in closely packed bands round a twig. The larvae are gregarious until pupation; elm is their preferred foodplant, though they will take willow, sallow, poplar, whitebeam, pear and cherry.

Peacock Butterfly *Inachis io* 60mm. Common in open fields, downland, woodland and wherever flowers grow, especially in gardens. Widespread in Europe, including Britain. Attracted to buddleia, lucerne, thistle, knapweed and marjoram; in woodland, congregates on hemp agrimony. Single brood; flies from July–September and again, after hibernation, from early March–May. Eggs are laid on the undersurface of a nettle leaf. Larvae live communally within a web of silk, moving to a new shelter as food demands; they disperse about a week before pupation and then, all at once, disappear to pupate in concealment. Sole larval foodplant is nettle.

Red Admiral *Vanessa atalanta* 60mm. Found in woodland clearings, open fields, downland and flowery gardens. Flies throughout Europe, including Britain. Strong migrant, spreading northwards from the Mediterranean each summer to breed. Multi-brooded. In autumn often seen feeding on rotting fruit; also visits ivy blossom until late in the year. Adults hibernate but few survive the winter in Britain. Eggs laid singly on nettle. The larva lives a solitary life in a 'leaf tent'; very variable, usually black and spiny, but often a shade of greenish-grey; foodplant mainly nettle.

Painted Lady *Vanessa cardui* 60mm. Flies in flowery places on downland, at woodland edges and in gardens. Occurs throughout Europe; survives winter only in extreme south. Fast flyer, particularly when disturbed, often returning to original spot. Continuously brooded; flight season April–October. Larva lives solitarily, concealed in a leaf drawn together with silk; black and spiny with a yellow stripe along the side; foodplant mainly thistle, but also burdock, viper's bugloss, mallow, stinging nettle, runner bean and *Helichrysum*.

Small Tortoiseshell *Aglais urticae* 42mm. Attracted by flowery places, especially gardens. One of the commonest British butterflies, especially from July–September. Occurs throughout Europe, but seldom as abundantly as in Britain. Sexes similar but female has fatter abdomen. Two to three broods; flying from early March–October, over-wintering as adults. Eggs laid in single mass, near the top of a nettle. Larvae gregarious in silken web; in the final instar they split into smaller groups and finally pupate away from their foodplant under an eave or windowsill; feed on stinging nettle, though hop has been used in captivity.

gen 1

gen 2

Comma Butterfly *Polygonia c-album* 40mm. Found throughout Europe in open spaces on the edges of woodlands, hedgerows and in gardens. The Comma is one butterfly whose range is spreading. Generally common, though local in northern regions. Two broods; flies March–September. Adults hibernate, selecting wild places. Eggs laid singly, or in small groups, on the upper surface of a leaf. Larva solitary, often beneath a leaf; in final instar has branched spines; the tail half is white and the larva sits curled up, greatly resembling a bird dropping; foodplant chiefly stinging nettle, but also elm, hop, sallow and gooseberry.

Map Butterfly *Araschnia levana* 42mm. Frequents rough ground and woody areas. This butterfly is common in central Europe but does not occur in Britain. So called because of its intricate map-like underside. Spring butterflies resemble a Fritillary; the summer brood (form *porosa*) look more like a miniature White Admiral. Flies April–September. The eggs are laid in strings, resembling catkins, on the underside of a nettle leaf. The larvae are gregarious and feed only on stinging nettle. Winter pupa; brown, very small and angular, sometimes with some markings in silver.

Cardinal Butterfly *Pandoriana pandora* 70mm. Frequents flowery meadows and woodland edges; loves thistle flowers and lime blossom. A southern European species found in Spain, southern and western France, Italy and eastwards to Greece. The largest European Fritillary, a fine species and powerful in flight. The underside colouring is bright pink and green, with attractive greenish suffusion on the top side in both sexes. Female has silver stripes. The eggs are laid singly on foodplant or nearby. Larva hibernates as soon as it hatches; striking coloration, black and spiny with two orange stripes along sides; foodplants wild pansy and violets.

Silver-washed Fritillary
Argynnis paphia 60mm. A woodland butterfly, common all over Europe though found only in south of Britain. Favours bramble blossom. Wing shape and wide markings distinguish the species. Male deep orange; female more greenish-buff. Female colour form (var. *valezina*) is distinct silvery-grey. Single brood; flies June–August. Eggs laid on oak or pine bark. Larva handsome, with long dark spines and two horns; remains on the bark when hatched, without feeding, throughout the winter; in spring, descends to feed on violet; pansy can be used in captivity.

Dark Green Fritillary
Mesoacidalia aglaia 60mm. Flies in flowery meadows, grassland, on coastal cliffs, dunes and in scrub. Found all over Europe, including Britain. Widespread and locally not uncommon. A very strong flier and well able to withstand strong winds in the exposed parts it inhabits; if blown off course, it swings round and continues flight with ease. There is one brood, flying July–August. Eggs are laid in July. Larva heavily spined, with red spots; on hatching, does not feed but hibernates; in spring lives solitarily, feeding on violet; pansy is accepted in captivity.

High Brown Fritillary
Fabriciana adippe 60mm. Frequents flowery meadows, woodland edges and uplands. Not uncommon in suitable habitat in central and southern Europe, but endangered in Britain. A notable variation is the form *cleodoxa*, which lacks silver spotting on the underside. Single brood, flying in July and August. Eggs are laid on the foodplant, dog violet, or nearby vegetation, with a preference for stems rather than leaves. Larva emerges in spring to feed, completing its growth in June; will also take sweet violet.

Niobe Fritillary *Fabriciana niobe* 42mm. Flies in flowery meadows and on mountainsides. Occurs in central and southern Europe, but not Britain. It is not rare in its habitat. Similar to the High Brown Fritillary, but does not have such strong markings and is noticeably smaller. Form *eris* occurs with no spots, and is an equivalent variety to form *cleodoxa* in the High Brown. In many parts, including Spain, only form *eris* is found. Single brood. Flight season June and July. Larva hibernates; foodplants violet and some plantains.

Queen of Spain Fritillary *Issoria lathonia* 42mm. Not uncommon in southern and eastern Europe, where it flies in flowery grassland and at the edges of woodland. As the Queen of Spain is migrant it can also be found in almost any type of habitat, and favours lucerne fields. Very rare migrant to Britain. Two or more broods, depending on geographical situation; flies from February–October. Winter larva usual but adults sometimes overwinter in the extreme south. Foodplants are violet and closely related plants.

Marbled Fritillary *Brenthis daphne* 40mm. Flies in sunny flower valleys and hills in southern and central Europe; does not occur in Britain, western Spain or Portugal. Not uncommon in its habitats. Can be distinguished by the underside of mottled lilac with brown and yellow. There is one brood; flight season June–August. The larva hibernates; larval foodplants are violet and bramble. The pupa is yellow or grey with red and gold spots.

Lesser Marbled Fritillary *Brenthis ino* 38mm. Damp grassland with flowers is the favoured habitat. This Fritillary is fairly widespread over Europe, excluding Britain and north-west France, but is thought to be declining because of land drainage. In Spain, it is found on the north coast and in the Madrid area. There is one brood; flight season June–August. The winter is passed as a larva. Larval foodplants are meadowsweet, great burnet and raspberry.

♂

♂ ♂

Shepherd's Fritillary *Boloria pales* 35mm. Occurs on mountain slopes over 1,500m in isolated patches in the Pyrenees, Alps, Balkans, Czechoslovakia, Poland, West Germany and Spain. It is locally common. Sometimes small groups are encountered well above the snow line, apparently oblivious of the Arctic conditions. Wing shape and markings distinctly angular in comparison with other *Boloria*. Very similar to *B. napaea* but markings more prominent and darker. There is one brood; flight season June–August. The larva hibernates; foodplant violet.

♂

♀ ♂

Small Pearl-bordered Fritillary *Clossiana selene* 40mm. Lives in open woodland; prefers moist areas. Occurs in northern and central Europe (excluding southern Spain, southern France and Italy). Not rare. Can be confused with Pearl-bordered but on underside has several silver spots in addition to border of seven pearls whilst *euphrosyne* has only two. Swift flapping flight, often gliding low. Generally one brood, flying June–July. In hot summers there can be a second brood, August–September. Eggs laid singly on dog violet. Larva hibernates when less than half grown; brown with two horn-like bristles behind head.

Pearl-bordered Fritillary *Clossiana euphrosyne* 42mm. A woodland species, particularly in large areas of deciduous forest; sometimes inhabits heathland. Found all over Europe except southern Spain. Not rare. Underside has two silver spots and a border of seven pearls (*see* Small Pearl-bordered). One brood is usual, flying May–June; in exceptionally hot weather, a second brood may occur in August. Eggs are laid on dog violet. Larva feeds before hibernation; black, flecked with white and spined.

Titania's Fritillary *Clossiana titania* 50mm. Occurs in light woodland, clearings and adjacent meadows. Range restricted and isolated. Found in parts of the Pyrenees, most of the Alps and part of the Baltic area. From the extreme east and south of Scandinavia and central Europe, its range extends widely across Russia and Asia. Locally not uncommon. Distinguished by bold and rather angular upperside markings, especially hindwing inner margin of fish-shaped spots; underside a characteristic purple with sharp markings; purple coloration stronger in the alpine race. Single brood; flies June–August. Larva hibernates; foodplants are violet and *Polygonum*.

Weaver's Fritillary *Clossiana dia* 35mm. Found in light woodland and scrub, this Fritillary is widely distributed across Europe from northern Spain, France and eastwards. It does not occur in Britain or the south tip of Italy. This is one of the smallest fritillaries, the underside distinguishing it from others with wide bands of dull purple, and angular patterning. There are two to three broods; flight season May–September. The eggs are laid on violet. The larva hibernates.

Glanville Fritillary *Melitaea cinxia* 40mm. Flies on open flowery slopes. In Britain found only in the Isle of Wight. Elsewhere not uncommon. Distributed widely in southern and central Europe; absent from southern Spain. Distinguished by five round black spots in the underside submarginal band. Usually two broods, flying May–June and August–September. Egg mass laid on plantains, on which larvae live gregariously in a web, later hibernating in a tight cluster. In spring the larvae feed openly, sometimes moving together in a wide black blanket, and have been known to spread onto roads.

Knapweed Fritillary *Melitaea phoebe* 50mm. Favours flowery fields and hillsides. Widely distributed and common in southern and central Europe; absent from Britain and southern Spain. Can be distinguished by large orange submarginal crescent in the third space of the forewings. On hindwings black spots in the underside orange submarginal band are occasionally present. Colouring and size very variable, especially in the female. At low levels there are two broods from April–August; in mountains only one brood, flying in July. Winter is passed in the larval stage; foodplants knapweed and sometimes plantain.

Spotted Fritillary *Melitaea didyma* 35–50mm. Flies on mountain slopes and in flowery meadows. Very widespread and quite common over central and southern Europe, up to 1,800m. Not found in Britain or northern France. Male a much deeper orange than the female. Both sexes extremely geographically variable. There are usually two broods, flying May–August, but only one at higher altitudes. Eggs laid in batches on foodplants, plantain, toadflax and speedwell. Larvae live gregariously until after hibernation.

False Heath Fritillary *Melitaea diamina* 40–48mm. Frequents shady grassland, especially with scattered trees. Widespread in southern and central Europe; not found in Britain, southern and central Spain or southern Greece. Upperside very dark, especially hindwings. On underside hindwing each crescent and orange submarginal band encloses a small, round spot. Generally single-brooded, flying in June and July. In southern regions there is an extended flight season with two broods. Eggs laid in batches on foodplants, plantain, cow-wheat and speedwell. Larvae live and hibernate gregariously in a web on the foodplant, separating in spring.

Heath Fritillary *Mellicta athalia* 44–48mm. Often common in flowery fields, open woods and woodland edges. Widely distributed over Europe except southern Spain. In Britain endangered, with only a few found in south-west. Lack of dark spots in submarginal band of crescents on underside hindwing distinguish Heath from other small fritillaries. One to three broods, May–September. Adults seldom seen singly, occurring in colonies which move with overgrowth and change of habitat. Eggs laid in batches. Larvae live gregariously in a loose web on cow-wheat, plantain, foxglove and wood sage, until dispersal for pupation.

Meadow Fritillary *Mellicta parthenoides* 40mm. Prefers damp meadows, especially on lower mountain slopes. Widespread in Spain, Portugal, France, range extending to Jura, south-west Bavaria and south-west Switzerland. Common in some localities. Distinguished by a black discal spot lying obliquely on the underside forewing. Upperside markings are thin and irregular. There are two broods at lower altitudes; flight seasons May–June and August–September. Larvae live gregariously and hibernate on plantain and cow-wheat.

Assmann's Fritillary *Mellicta britomartis* 35mm. Flies on flowery heaths and in grassland meadows. An east European species occurring in the Balkans, northwards to Hungary, Poland and south-west Sweden. Very local. Much resembles the Meadow Fritillary; both are so variable that confident identification is only possible from genitalia examination. Two broods in southern part of the range, flying from May–September. Eggs laid in batches on plantain and speedwell. Larvae live and hibernate gregariously in a web.

Scarce Fritillary *Hypodryas maturna* 44–50mm. Flies in open woodland and along valley bottoms. Range widely scattered in central and eastern Europe. To the south, flies in Greece and southern Balkans. A band occurs from near Paris, eastwards across northern Germany and Poland and south to Austria. A third area occurs in southern Sweden. Very localised; not uncommon in some restricted places. Attracted to privet blossom. Much deeper orange than Marsh Fritillary. Single brood; flies May–June. Larvae gregarious on ash, poplar and beech in autumn; solitary after hibernation on plantain, scabious and speedwell.

Cynthia's Fritillary *Hypodryas cynthia* 42–50mm. Flies on mountain heaths with juniper and blueberry, in scrub and grassland. Restricted to the Alps and to an area in Bulgaria. Very scarce and local. The male is instantly recognisable by its unique white patterning. The female is larger, without white, a soft orange with low contrasting pattern. Single brood; flies in July, usually at altitudes above 2,000m. Eggs are laid in scattered batches on plantain and lady's mantle. The larvae feed and hibernate gregariously.

Marsh Fritillary *Eurodryas aurinia* 40–52mm. By no means only a marsh species, often found on chalk and high ground. Flies in flowery meadows, moors and boggy margins of lakes. Becoming endangered in Europe; possibly commonest in Britain but still very local. Occurs throughout Europe except northern Scandinavia. Hindwing submarginal orange band well developed, with well defined black spot in each space. Single brood; flies April–July. Eggs laid in large cluster on devil's bit scabious and plantain. Larvae gregarious and hibernate tightly clustered at base of foodplant; will feed on wild honeysuckle in captivity.

Marbled White *Melanargia galathea* 50mm. Lives in colonies on grassland; often abundant; attracted to knapweed, scabious and thistle. Absent from Scandinavia, otherwise found throughout the rest of Europe including southern Britain. There is considerable local variation. The Spanish race, form *lachesis*, has a broad white basal area, lacking the black markings close to the body. Female form (*leucomelas*) has underside hindwing totally white. Much natural variation in the markings and ground colour. One brood, flying from June–September. The larva overwinters at the base of the grasses on which it feeds.

Esper's Marbled White *Melanargia russiae* 50mm. Found in upland and mountain meadows, not usually below 1,000m altitude. Confined to parts of the most southerly European countries. Absent from north and west Spain; its eastward range includes south-west France, much of Italy and parts of Greece. There are several similar species. The underside hindwings have larger marginal spots than those of the Marbled White but natural variation makes it impossible to list specific identification marks. There is one brood; the butterflies are seen in June and July. The larva feeds on grasses and hibernates.

Woodland Grayling *Hipparchia fagi* 70mm. This species occurs in woodland clearings and sparse woods. Well distributed and not uncommon from northern France and eastwards to Greece. Absent from Britain and Scandinavia; although found otherwise throughout southern Europe, does not occur in most of Spain. Confusion with the Rock Grayling (which does occur in Spain) will only occur in parts of southern France and central Europe (Austria and Czechoslovakia). The female has a broader hindwing white band than the male. Single brooded; flies July and August. Larva hibernates at the base of its grass foodplants.

Rock Grayling *Hipparchia alcyone* 60mm. A butterfly of mountain slopes and dried-up river beds. Found throughout the Iberian peninsula, the south of France, in Austria, Czechoslovakia and northwards to Latvia. Not rare where it occurs. Does not seem to be affected by very dry seasons when other species are noticeably scarcer. Smaller than the Woodland Grayling. The butterflies adopt the typical Grayling resting attitude, tilting away from the sun, thereby casting no shadow and melting completely into the surrounding background of rock and soil. Single brooded; flight season June and July. Larva is a grass feeder and hibernates.

Grayling *Hipparchia semele* 50mm. Favours stony and rocky places, cliffs and heathland. The only Grayling occurring in Britain; its range is throughout the whole of Europe, except for some of the Mediterranean islands. There are small races, sometimes as little as half the normal size. The wings are seldom seen open except in courtship. Single brooded; the butterflies are seen from June (July in northern Europe) to August. The larva is a grass feeder and hibernates. Pupates in a loose cocoon, producing a chrysalis that is, like a moth pupa, unattached and a smooth, shining brown.

Tree Grayling *Hipparchia statilinus* 50mm. A lowland species that flies in rocky places but is particularly associated with trees, in which it often rests. Absent from Britain and most of Scandinavia, but is found commonly throughout the rest of Europe. Its dark colouring might be confused with that of the Dryad, but in all other respects it is marked like a Grayling. There is one brood, on the wing from July–September. The larva hibernates amongst its grass foodplants.

Hermit *Chazara briseis* 50–60mm. Dry, rocky places are the habitat for the Hermit, even up to 2,000m. Although a southern European butterfly, its range extends north to Brittany, but it is not found as far north as Britain; absent from western Iberia. Not rare but seldom seen in great numbers. The size is very variable. Its clear, white bands distinguish the species and its smaller size separates it from the otherwise similar Great Banded Grayling. Single brood; flies June and July. The larva is a grass feeder and hibernates.

Alpine Grayling *Oenis glacialis* 50mm. Restricted to high mountains at altitudes around 1,800m in the French and Italian Alps and just into Austria. Though not a rarity, seldom encountered. The Alpine Grayling is really an Arctic species, from an evolutionary point of view; all its *Oenis* relatives are found in the Arctic Circle. Like these, it is pallid in its colour and markings, unlike the other Graylings. Its flight season is short, occurring in June and July. The larva feeds on grasses, hibernating amongst the roots, covered with snow for much of its life.

Dryad *Minois dryas* 60mm. Found in open country and grassland, sometimes bordering woodland. The range is in a band across central Europe, excluding most of Spain and Italy in the south; does not occur in Britain or Scandinavia. Common in places from sea level up to 1,000m or more. Notable for its dark colouring and large, rounded wings. The female is larger and much less dark than the male; her eye-spots are larger and more prominent. One brood; flight season June–August. The larva feeds on grasses, amongst which it hibernates.

Great Banded Grayling *Brintesia circe* 60–70mm. One of the largest of the Satyrids, this striking butterfly is found in fields, woodland edges and open country, from southern Europe up to the north of France and eastwards to Greece and beyond. Common, though occurring singly, both at low altitudes and in mountains. The size and clear, white band ensure its identification. Although possibly confusable with the White Admiral, its habitat is quite different and the underside is clearly that of a Grayling. There is one brood; flies June–August. The larva feeds on grasses and hibernates.

False Grayling *Arethusana arethusa* 40–50mm. Wild, open grassland is the home of the False Grayling. It occurs in scattered, local colonies over a wide area of central Europe, from northern France, southwards to Spain, and eastwards to Austria and Czechoslovakia. Absent from Portugal and most of Italy. Those found in the eastern regions are smaller and have much less orange marking. There is one brood; flight season July and August. The larva is a grass feeder and hibernates.

Arran Brown *Erebia ligea* 50mm. A mountain and Arctic butterfly, found in grassland, usually amongst conifers, from low level up to some 1,500m. Occurs in southern Sweden and from the Alps and Jura Mountains eastwards almost throughout Europe. Reputed occurrence on the isle of Arran but not now found in Britain. Common in places; lives in colonies. Easily recognised by its size, clear orange-eyed bands and the distinct white hindwing band on the underside. Female rounder and paler than male. One brood, flying in July. The larva feeds on grasses and hibernates.

Large Ringlet *Erebia euryale* 40mm. Occurs in light conifer woodland, amongst the grasses. The range follows mountain regions (1,000–2,000m) from northern Spain, across central and southern France, the Alps and into Greece. Rather similar to the Arran Brown but it is smaller and its markings are not as rich, though there is some natural variation. In the Italian Alps the markings are so reduced as to be hardly recognisable. The male also lacks the sex brands seen on the Arran Brown. One brood; flies July–August. The larva feeds on grasses and hibernates.

Small Mountain Ringlet *Erebia epiphron* 32mm. A high altitude butterfly of craggy slopes. One of the smaller *Erebias* and one of just two occurring in Britain, where it is found locally in parts of the Lake District and in Scotland. Exists in scattered localities from northern Spain, across France and the Alps to Yugoslavia and further east. Extremely variable, there are several named forms. Distinctive characteristics have many exceptions but, in general, *epiphron* has more distinctly pupilled eye-spots than others of similar size and underside marking. Single brood; flies July–August. The larva feeds on grasses and hibernates.

Scotch Argus *Erebia aethiops* 40mm. Found on high ground. In Britain occurs in extreme north and widely in Scotland, late July–September. Found in central France; eastwards from the Jura and Alps, north and southwards to Lithuania, and to Balkans, Greece and beyond; absent from Spain and Pyrenees. Its brick-red bands are more prominent and defined than most other *Erebias* of this size, though less so than Arran Brown and Large Ringlet, but it lacks the white-dotted fringes that are found in these two species. Single brood. Larva a grass feeder and hibernates.

Woodland Ringlet *Erebia medusa* 40mm. Less of a high-altitude species than many of the *Erebias*, except in southern areas. Its range is similar to that of the Scotch Argus (though it is absent from Britain), occurring from central France in a wide fan eastwards. Often common. Can be confused with the Almond-eyed Ringlet but it is earlier in the start of its season and its range coincides only in certain localities. Single brood, flight season May–June. The larva is grass-feeding and hibernates.

Almond-eyed Ringlet *Erebia alberganus* 40mm. At medium to high altitudes, some 1,200m to 1,800m, this species is often common in Alpine meadows and on rocky slopes. Its range is very limited to small areas of northern Spain (not in the Pyrenees), the southern French Alps, Switzerland, northern Italy and the Apennines. Its name describes its distinguishing features with the orange bands broken into pupilled ovals. However, this and all the *Erebias* are so variable that sure identification is very difficult. There is one brood, flying in June and July. The larva feeds on grasses and hibernates.

Piedmont Ringlet *Erebia meolans* 50mm. High Alpine meadows up to 2,000m are the home of this species. It occurs in northern and central Spain, the Pyrenees, a wide area of the Alps from France and Italy up to southern Germany and into Austria; also found in central Italy. Spanish specimens are very dark and brightly marked. There are other widely differing named subspecies which make identification extremely difficult. The Swiss form is smaller and with much reduced orange bands. There is one brood, flying from late June into July. The larva feeds on grasses and hibernates.

Meadow Brown *Maniola jurtina* 50mm. A grassland species of lowlands up to 1,500m or more, occurring in colonies of some density. Probably Europe's commonest butterfly, found throughout, up to central Scandinavia. Much natural variation in both colour and size. Male either partially or totally lacks the orange forewing patch seen in the female; tends to be darker and smaller. Subspecies *hispula* has well defined and brighter orange patches; occurs in Ireland, some Scottish isles, Isle of Man, western France and Spain. Single brood; long flight season May–September, depending on latitude. The larva feeds on grasses and hibernates.

Dusky Meadow Brown *Hyponephele lycaon* 40mm. Found in dry, rocky places, rather than in meadows. Range nearly as extensive as that of the Meadow Brown, but it is absent from Portugal, northern France, Britain and Scandinavia. Can be distinguished from Meadow Brown by smaller size, more forewing orange in male and two forewing eye-spots in female. One brood; flight season from late June into August. The larva feeds on grasses and hibernates.

Ringlet *Aphantopus hyperantus* 48mm. Often seen in woodland, the Ringlet frequents grassy places, particularly in damp areas. Really a lowland butterfly but occurs up to around 1,500m. Its range includes most of Europe, including Britain, but it is absent from south-west Iberia, southern France, Italy and northern Scandinavia. Not rare, but uncommon compared with the Meadow Brown. Distinguished by its dark, nearly black colouring, especially the male. There is a single brood, flying in June and July. The larva feed on grasses and hibernates.

Gatekeeper *Pyronia tithonus* 40mm. Also known as the Small Meadow Brown. Very common in places, favouring lanes and byways, sometimes meadows and downland; not a butterfly of high altitudes. Greatly attracted to certain flowers, especially marjoram and ragwort, on which it is often seen in groups. Occurs throughout Europe except northern Britain and Scandinavia. Variable in size and colour density. Male distinguished by prominent area of dark scent scales on forewing; smaller than female. Single brood, flight season July–August. The larva feeds on grasses and hibernates.

Southern Gatekeeper *Pyronia cecelia* 35mm. Rough, rocky Mediterranean places are favoured by this species, from sea level up to the highest mountains. Range covers Spain, along the south coast of France, Italy and the coast of Yugoslavia. Often common. Smaller and brighter than the Gatekeeper; well defined markings with chalky areas on underside hindwing. Male forewing scent patch partitioned by veins. There are two broods; flight season May–August. The larva feeds on grasses and hibernates.

Spanish Gatekeeper *Pyronia bathseba* 35–50mm. This butterfly is found in sparse woodland, amongst conifers and on dry, rocky ground, usually at low altitudes. Its range covers Spain, the Pyrenees, southern and south-east France. Distinguished by the cream band across the underside hindwing (broad in the female) in both sexes. The female is much larger than the male. There are almost certainly two broods. This species is seen earlier than its relatives, flying April–July. The larva feeds on grasses and hibernates.

Large Heath *Coenonympha tullia* 38mm. Moorland and open grasslands are the habitat of this species. Occurs in northern Europe, including northern Britain where it is local and uncommon, southwards to central France and the Alps, eastwards into Russia. One of several *Coenonympha* that can easily be confused. There are distinct geographical forms, the Scottish being particularly light in colouring. There is a single brood; flight season late June–July. The larva feeds on grasses and hibernates.

Small Heath *Coenonympha pamphilus* 30mm. A very common species seen in grassland from sea level to some altitude. Found throughout Europe from April (May in Britain and the north) to September. Distinguished from other Heaths by its smaller size. The sexes are similar but the female abdomen is fatter and the wings are more rounded. Colour varies from orange to ochre according to race and freshness. There are usually two broods. The larva feeds and hibernates on grasses.

♂

♂

Pearly Heath *Coenonympha arcania* 35mm. Locally common in grassland, on grassy slopes, usually in valleys but sometimes found up to 1,800m, and even at woodland edges. It is very widely distributed throughout most of Europe except the greater part of Spain, Britain and most of Scandinavia. More orange than the Large and most other Heaths. There is a single brood; flies June and July. The larva feeds and hibernates on grasses.

Alpine Heath *Coenonympha gardetta* 33mm. Often locally common in flowery grassland at high altitudes but occurs in a rather restricted Alpine range, from the French Alps, through Switzerland to Austria and Italy. The forewing eye-spots are reduced or even absent. Heavily suffused with brown and olive green. The underside hindwing white band distinguishes the Alpine Heath, being broad and prominent. There is a single brood, flying in June and July. The larva feeds on grasses and hibernates.

Chestnut Heath *Coenonympha glycerion* 35mm. A mountain butterfly of grassy slopes at altitudes above and below 1,000m. Found in the Pyrenees, northern Spain, French mountain regions and eastward to Italy and all of mountainous east Europe. Forewings clear orange-buff; there is a prominent band of underside hindwing spots but forewing eye-spot is usually missing or small. The lack of the underside hindwing white band helps to identify the species. There is one brood, flying in June and July. The larva feeds on grasses and hibernates.

Speckled Wood *Pararge aegeria* 45mm. A common butterfly of woodland rides and edges, lightly wooded gardens and grassy places. Occurs throughout Europe, including Britain, but only in southern Scandinavia. In southern Europe the ground colour is orange, instead of the pale cream markings found from south and central France northwards. Male has forewing scent brand, more angular wings and less open markings than female. Successive broods from April (March in south) until October. Hibernation is sometimes as larva, sometimes as pupa. The larva is a grass feeder.

Wall Brown *Lasiommata megera* 45mm. Favours dry, rocky grassland with bare soil patches. Flies from sea level to over 1,000m. Its range includes all of Europe except northern Britain and most of Scandinavia. Common but solitary. Its habitat and curious habit of accompanying a walker are clues to the Wall's identity. Possibly confusable with a Fritillary or the orange form of Speckled Wood. Male forewing sex brands prominent; female has more rounded wings and more open orange patterning. There are two broods or more, flying from May–September (March in southern countries). Hibernation is in larval stage. The larva feeds on grasses.

Large Wall Brown *Lasiommata maera* 45–50mm. Often common in open countryside and on rocky slopes, from sea level to over 1,600m. Found throughout Europe except in Britain and extreme north Scandinavia. Southern specimens have much more orange wings, but basal areas of brown, as well as the butterfly's size, distinguish it from the Wall Brown. North of the Alps it is smaller and has much less orange marking. Two broods in the south, flying from June–September; a single brood in the north, from late June–early August. The larva feeds on grasses and hibernates.

Northern Wall Brown
Lasiommata petropolitana 40mm. In Scandinavia, flies at low levels and in mountains, often common among conifers and in damp places. Further south, it occurs high in mountains (around 2,000m) in the Pyrenees, high Alps, the Balkans and Greece. Rather similar to the Large Wall Brown but smaller and usually found in different localities. Probably a single brood, flying from May–July. The larva hibernates, often under snow, at the base of the grasses on which it feeds.

Woodland Brown *Lopinga achine* 50mm. Not common but found in widely scattered woodland localities across central Europe. A low level butterfly, seldom seen above 800m. Absent from Britain and Scandinavia. Found in a part of northern Spain but otherwise not south of a line running across the south of France, north of the Mediterranean coast. Larger than the Ringlet and has rows of much larger eye-spots. Female similar to male but may have rather larger spots and more rounded wings. Single brood; flies mainly in June. The larva is a grass feeder and hibernates.

Duke of Burgundy Fritillary *Hamearis lucina* 30mm. Flies in fields and open woodland but depends on presence of the larval foodplants primrose and cowslip. Usually lowland but may be found up to 1,000m. Range covers most of Europe, including England; absent from Spain except in north, Holland, north Germany and Scandinavia except in south. Lives in colonies; local and rather scarce. Not a true Fritillary. Female wings more rounded with more open markings than male, especially on hindwings. Single brood, except in southern Europe. Flies from May; seen as late as August in southern regions. Pupa hibernates.

Brown Hairstreak *Thecla betulae* 40–50mm. Frequents hedges of blackthorn and light woodland; not usually found on high ground. Occurs throughout most of Europe, including southern England, but in only a few scattered Spanish localities; absent from all but the southern tip of Scandinavia. Though widely distributed, seldom noticed and considered to be uncommon. Female easily distinguished by orange forewing band. Single brood; flies July–August. Eggs are laid in the fork of blackthorn twigs where they remain throughout the winter. Many are lost through winter hedge cutting by farmers.

Purple Hairstreak *Quercusia quercus* 38mm. Lives in colonies in oak woods, sometimes quite commonly. Usually a lowland butterfly, except in southern Europe. Range extends almost throughout the Continent, including Britain and southern Scandinavia. In Spain, subspecies *iberica* has a pale underside, often without the pale stripe. The male is dark iridescent purple all over; the female has a bright purple forewing patch. Single brood, flying June–July. Eggs are laid usually against a bud of the foodplant, oak, or in a fork of a twig, where they remain for the winter. Ash is also recorded as a foodplant.

Spanish Purple Hairstreak *Laeosopis roboris* 40mm. Usually found in the vicinity of ash trees. Restricted to the Iberian peninsula and a small part of the French south-west Mediterranean coast. Rather uncommon, it flies from sea level to altitudes above 1,000m. The female has strong but small purple patches on the forewing. In the male, the purple colouring covers most of the forewing. The underside is contrastingly coloured with bright orange marginal bands on greyish ochre. Single brood, flying May–July. Eggs are laid on the twigs of the foodplant where they remain for the winter.

Sloe Hairstreak *Nordmannia acaciae* 30mm. Rather local, this species is found usually within reach of blackthorn bushes, from low altitudes to low mountain regions. The range stretches in a horizontal band across Europe, from central France and Spain, through the Alps into Czechoslovakia and beyond. Its small size helps to identify the species, but males, in particular, could be mistaken for any of four allied species. Nearest in appearance is the False Ilex Hairstreak which occurs only in Spain. There is only one brood, flying June–July. Eggs are laid on blackthorn twigs and remain for the winter.

Ilex Hairstreak *Nordmannia ilicis* 35mm. Commonest in the south, but local on rough, open land supporting oaks and oak scrub. Very wide range across most of Europe but absent from Britain and almost all of Scandinavia. The female has a large orange forewing area, with little or no orange on the hindwing (distinguishing the species from the Blue Spot and Black Hairstreaks which have orange hindwing patches). Single brood; flies from sea level to 1,500m during June and July. Eggs are laid often on small oak bushes and here they remain for the winter.

False Ilex Hairstreak
Nordmannia esculi 35mm. Found in areas of rough scrubby ground with smaller oak trees and bushes. Restricted to Spain, the Pyrenees and extreme south-west of France. Rather local. Hindwing streak mark faint or nearly absent. Male underside markings less prominent than the similar Sloe Hairstreak; lacks the prominent, deep orange spot at the anal angle on the underside, found in the Ilex. Female lacks orange forewing patch and has pale, lightly marked underside. Single brood, flying June–July. Eggs are laid on the foodplant (oak spp) and overwinter.

Blue Spot Hairstreak
Strymonidia spini 35mm. Found in rough scrub, open country and at woodland edges, from low level to over 1,500m. Range extends widely across Europe but excludes Britain and extreme northern countries; absent from Scandinavia. Rather local and becoming scarce. Both sexes distinguished by prominent blue hindwing spot on underside anal angle. Male has oval scent brand above forewing cell (not found on similar species except for White Letter Hairstreak). Female has broad areas of orange on forewing/hindwing. Single brood, flying June–July. Eggs are laid on the foodplants, blackthorn and buckthorn, and overwinter.

White Letter Hairstreak *Strymonidia w-album* 35mm. A butterfly of hedgerows and woodland edges, sometimes colonising trees of the foodplant, elm and wych elm. Local and very scattered, declining since Dutch Elm disease. Range covers most of Europe, including Britain; rare and very scattered in northern Spain, absent further south in the peninsula; occurs in southern Scandinavia only. Hindwing streak more prominent than other similar species. Male has oval scent brand above the cell (distinguishing it from otherwise similar female and other species except Black Hairstreak). Single brood; flies in July. Eggs are laid on the foodplant and overwinter.

Black Hairstreak *Strymonidia pruni* 35mm. Found in open woodland in the vicinity of the larval foodplant, blackthorn; also attracted to privet and bramble blossom. In Britain, restricted to a few woods in Buckinghamshire and Oxfordshire. Found in northern Spain, southern France, broadly fanning north and south in an easterly direction to cover central Europe into the Balkans, Greece and Russia; absent from southern Spain, Italy, northern France, Benelux and most of Scandinavia. Local or very rare. Forewing underside orange marginal band distinguishes it from similar species. Single brood; flies in July. Eggs are laid on blackthorn and overwinter.

Green Hairstreak *Callophrys rubi* 25mm. Occurs at edges of woodland, amongst bushes and hedgerows, even in grassland if invaded by bushes and on rough mountain slopes to 1,800m or more. Found throughout Europe; local, sometimes common. Single brood; flies as early as March in southern Europe, otherwise May–June. Larvae are cannibalistic so must be segregated when reared. Foodplants for this species are extremely varied and include, among many others, gorse, rock rose, dogwood, trefoils, buckthorn, whortleberry, oak, heather and runner bean. Unlike any other Hairstreak, winter is passed in the pupal stage.

Provence Hairstreak *Tomares ballus* 25mm. Found on rough ground and in low mountains. Not very appropriately named; this butterfly's stronghold is in central and southern Spain, though it occurs also on the neighbouring Mediterranean coast of France. Scarce and local. In appearance this curiosity has, on the upperside, strong characteristics of the Coppers and, on the underside, some of the appearances of Hairstreaks. Flies as early as January, until April, in Spain. The foodplant is bird's foot trefoil. The dormant period (late summer and autumn) is spent in the pupal stage.

Lycaenids

Violet Copper *Lycaena helle*
30mm. A butterfly of damp meadows, moorland and bogs, sometimes in mountains; lives in small colonies. It has a curious and scattered distribution, with a narrow band starting in south-west France, eastwards towards the Alps, broadening northwards into the Jura and Germany, and eastwards again to Switzerland, Czechoslovakia and Poland; additionally found in central and northern Scandinavia. Scarce and very local. The violet iridescence is seen only in the male. Single brood, flying May–July. Larva feeds on bistort, knotgrass and sorrel. Pupa overwinters, buried amongst debris.

Small Copper *Lycaena phlaeas*
30–38mm. Typically, individuals are found in dry, waste ground but are also seen in flowery meadows and gardens. Altitude may be from sea level up to as much as 2,000m. Range encompasses the whole of Europe and habitat is widely variable. Common, though found singly. Size rather variable, larger and brighter butterflies are found in southern Europe. Male has a more accentuated hindwing point or tail and more angular wings. At least two broods; flight period April (in south) until October. Larva feeds on docks and sorrels and hibernates at the base of the foodplants.

Large Copper *Lycaena dispar* 35–50mm. *L. dispar rutilus* is the most usually encountered race. Inhabits flowery, damp meadows or rough ground, often in mountains. Found in eastern France and throughout central Europe, eastwards. Alpine specimens are small; those found in Poland are large and rich in colouring, approaching the scarce Dutch race *L. dispar batavus*, which is established in Britain at Woodwalton Reserve, Cambridgeshire. Foodplants are great water dock, other docks, sorrels and bistort. *Rutilus* generally has two broods, flying May–September; *batavus* usually only one, flying July. Larva overwinters at base of foodplant, often submerged.

Scarce Copper *Heodes virgaureae* 28–40mm. Not uncommon in grassy meadows, often in mountains. Range extensive; found in north and central Spain, Pyrenees and eastwards into most of Europe, excluding west and north France, Benelux and Britain. Several subspecies, and considerable geographical variation in both size and marking. Underside broken white line distinguishes the species but in Spain the line is vestigial. The spotted female is confusable with the female Sooty Copper but is larger and underside differs. Single brood; flies July–August. The larva feeds on sorrels and docks; overwinters fully formed, unhatched, within the eggshell.

Lycaenids

Sooty Copper *Heodes tityrus* 30–35mm. Open country and flowery meadows are the habitats for this species. Distribution is wide, covering most of Europe except southern Spain and Portugal, Britain and most of Scandinavia. Colonies scattered, sometimes not rare, but butterflies encountered individually as a rule. Several subspecies, notably high altitude Alpine *subalpinus* in which upperside is black and almost devoid of markings. Typical female has orange forewing, spotted with black; male has only an orange marginal band. Two broods, flying April–May and August–September. Larva feeds on sorrels and docks on which it hibernates.

Purple-shot Copper *Heodes alciphron* 40mm. Occurs in flowery meadows both at low level and well into mountain regions. Range covers greater part of Europe but excludes north-west, Britain and Scandinavia. Local, sometimes common. The more northern races (Germany, Jura, Poland and central Europe) have a strong, iridescent purple flush on male; female darkly suffused brown. Southern race (*H.a. gordius*), found in the Alps, Pyrenees and Spain, is slightly larger, bright orange ground colour in both sexes with slight purple flush on male. Single brood, flying in June–July. Larva feeds on sorrels and docks, on which it hibernates.

Purple-edged Copper *Palaeochrysophanus hippothoe* 32–40mm. Flies in flowery meadows at practically all but highest mountain levels. Widely distributed throughout Europe (into the furthest north of Norway), excluding southern Spain, west and north France and Britain. Often common. Geographically variable, especially female, which can be so suffused at high altitudes as to be almost devoid of marking. At least five named races. Single brood, flying June–July; in the south-east there is a very large race that may have another brood. The larva overwinters at the foot of the foodplants, bistorts and docks.

Long-tailed Blue *Lampides boeticus* 35mm. Strong migrant, whose natural home is in southern Europe, North Africa and right across Asia. Not uncommon from Alps southwards; above this line migration occurs and the butterflies might be found in almost any type of habitat, especially open ground, meadows and flowering crops such as lucerne and lavender. Migration reaches the north coast of Europe and rarely into Britain but seldom further north. Continuously brooded; found May–October. The larva feeds on the buds and seed-pods of gorse, lupin, bladder senna and related Papilionaceae.

Lang's Short-tailed Blue *Syntarucus pirithous* 30mm. Seen on dry hillsides and open ground, flitting about close to the ground and resting among the rocks. Distribution ranges from Spain to Greece along the entire south coast of Europe, where it is often common. Migration to the north coast of Europe occurs each summer, the butterflies becoming very scarce in the north and stopping short of Britain. Smaller than Long-tailed Blue and with more detailed underside patterning. Female is more heavily patterned than male. Continuously brooded, flying from at least March–October. The larva feeds on broom, lucerne and other Papilionaceae.

Short-tailed Blue *Everes argiades* 30mm. Very local in widely scattered colonies, but a colony may contain considerable numbers and it can be locally common in quite a small area. Occurs from northern Spain up to Brittany and eastwards to Russia. On the British List but exceedingly rare migrant. Commonest in the south; northern examples would appear to be migrants. The male is violet blue; female is often larger and nearly black. Smaller and more violet than either of the other Short-tailed Blues. Two broods, flying throughout the summer. Larva feeds on trefoils, vetches, gorse and allied plants.

Small Blue *Cupido minimus* 25mm. Often on chalk and limestone, very local and scattered in flowery grassland. Range extends throughout Europe, including Britain, except southern Spain and northern Scandinavia. Tends to live in small pockets, not straying over a wide area. Sexes similar charcoal colour but male has dusting of gunmetal-blue scales, particularly in the basal areas. Can be confused with Short-tailed Blue but has no tails. Single brood; flies June–July (earlier in south). Larval foodplant kidney vetch and probably other vetches. Larva hibernates, unusually, in its final instar, concealed in a hibernaculum like a flimsy cocoon.

Holly Blue *Celastrina argiolus* 30mm. Very often a garden species; woodland rides and edges, walls and inland cliff faces are all potential habitats because of its breeding habits on ivy and holly. Usually encountered singly but small groups may be observed on ivy blossom in summer. Range extends across Europe, including Britain, excepting only north of Scotland and north Norway. Female distinguished by black margin and apex which is stronger in the second generation. First brood eggs laid on holly; summer brood on ivy; buckthorn, gorse and other shrubs may also be used. Pupa hibernates.

Green-underside Blue *Glaucopsyche alexis* 35mm. Flowery grassland slopes are the chief habitat, usually on uplands to 1,000m and over. Widely distributed across most of Europe, excluding eastern Iberia, Britain and all but the south of Scandinavia. Not usually common; becoming scarcer. Female distinguished by her brown colouring. Bands of bold underside spots, especially on forewing, identify this species, together with the greenish basal area. Larval foodplants are vetches, brooms and other Papilionaceae.

Alcon Blue *Maculinea alcon* 38mm. Distribution determined by that of larval foodplant, marsh gentian, which is restricted to boggy heathland. Mostly encountered in Germany, but occurs in northern Spain, France and eastwards throughout most of Europe, except for Britain and Scandinavia. Rare and endangered. Distinguished from similar species by paucity of spotting but in this and the ground colour, the species is geographically variable. Single brooded; flies in July. In third instar the larva is taken into an ants' nest where it lives through the winter and eventually pupates.

Large Blue *Maculinea arion* 40mm. Mostly found on grassy banks; coastal cliffs also typical habitat. Colonies widely scattered but may be numerous in certain areas. Range extends from northern Spain, across central France eastwards throughout Europe. Declared extinct in Britain in 1979 but reintroduced since. Absent from Scandinavia except for southern Sweden. Local; common in a few places mainly in July. Adults frequently encountered on larval foodplant, marjoram, in western Europe, thyme in other areas. Geographically variable, especially in mountains. In third instar, larva taken into an ants' nest where it feeds on brood and pupates in spring.

Scarce Large Blue *Maculinea teleius* 38mm. Flies in damp meadows, sometimes as high as 1,800m. Range extends from eastern France in a band eastwards, taking in Switzerland, Austria and Czechoslovakia; absent from Balkans. Local and very scarce. Distinguished from the Large Blue by smaller size of wings and spotting, and by underside colour which is deeper grey with almost no blue basal dusting. Female darker than male, with more pronounced spotting. Larva feeds for first two instars on great burnet and bird's foot trefoil, then in an ants' nest for the winter.

Dusky Large Blue *Maculinea nausithous* 40mm. Mostly a lowland species, found in marshy areas and lakeland borders. Range extends in a rather narrow band from the French Savoie Alps eastwards through Czechoslovakia and beyond. Local and usually scarce. Its very dark colouring, on both upper and underside, instantly distinguishes the species from the other Large Blues. Single brood; the butterflies are seen in June. The larva feeds for two instars on great burnet, afterwards in an ants' nest through the winter until pupation in spring.

Baton Blue *Pseudophilotes baton* 25mm. A mountain species, flying at altitudes up to 1,800m on flowery banks where the larval foodplant, wild thyme, grows. The range covers northern Spain, mountain areas of France and eastwards, excluding north Europe and the British Isles. The boldly speckled underside identifies the species, which is smaller than the Chequered Blue and is otherwise similar only to species that are very restricted in locality and hardly overlap. When double brooded, flies April–May and August–September. Winter is spent as a pupa where there is only one brood, otherwise as a larva.

Chequered Blue *Scolitantides orion* 30mm. Flies in low mountain regions on rough ground and slopes where the larval foodplants, stonecrop and other *Sedum* species grow. Widely separated races occur in Sweden and in parts of eastern Spain, southern France and northern Italy, in a narrow west-east band which then broadens into the Balkans. There may be one or two broods, flying from May–July. The female is more darkly suffused than the male. Winter is usually spent as a pupa but possibly also as the larva.

Silver-studded Blue *Plebejus argus* 24–30mm. Often in heathland but usually on grassy slopes. The range extends across all of Europe except for Scotland and northern Norway. Widely distributed but very local. There are several races and widely differing geographical forms. Some Spanish examples are twice the size of smaller northern races. Females are brown (except for extreme aberrant forms), males are blue. The number of broods ranges from one to three, depending on latitude. The flight season is approximately May–August. Larva feeds on trefoils, medick, sainfoin and other Papilionaceae. Winter is passed in the egg stage.

Idas Blue *Lycaeides idas* 25–30mm. An often common grassland butterfly. Widespread throughout most of Europe; absent only from western Iberia and Britain. Difficult to distinguish from Silver-studded Blue, because both species very variable, but the front tibia of Idas is spineless. Female normally brown, but in Arctic and certain southern regions has much blue colouring. Period and number of broods varies with latitude; flies mainly June–July. The larva feeds on vetches, lucerne and related Papilionaceae; spends the winter in an ants' nest. Summer pupa formed amongst ant brood.

Reverdin's Blue *Lycaeides argyrogonomon* 30mm. Meadows and grassland habitat are favoured by this species. Occurs in central France and eastwards throughout central and southern Europe; not found in Spain, western and northern Europe, including Britain and Scandinavia (except southern Sweden). Rather local. Difficult to distinguish from Silver-studded or Idas Blues. Underside metallic crescent marks on the orange submarginal band are often more pronounced than in Silver-studded. Usually two broods; flies May–September. The larva feeds on vetches and related small Papilionaceae. Winter egg or occasionally larva.

Cranberry Blue *Vacciniina optilete* 25mm. Associated with the larval foodplant, cranberry, this species flies on moorland and bogs, at the edges of scrubby woodland and sometimes at high altitude in Alpine regions. Range includes all Scandinavia and south into central Europe only as far as the Alps. Often common in Norway and Sweden. The violet-blue of the male is characteristic of this species and helps in identification; the strong grey underside is also a distinguishing feature. Single brood; flies in July. The larva hibernates while half grown.

Geranium Argus *Eumedonia eumedon* 30mm. Flies in flowery grassland, either at low level or in mountains according to area and latitude. In Scandinavia this is a lowland species. While its main stronghold is in central and eastern Europe and Scandinavia, fragmented colonies are also found in Italy, the Alps, south-west France and northern Spain. Scarce, perhaps rare. Sexes similar; upperside nearly black; underside usually has a pale wedge extending from discoidal spot. Single brood; flies in July. The larva feeds on cranesbill and related *Geranium* species, hibernates.

Brown Argus *Aricia agestis* 25mm. Occurs on downland, especially in southern Britain, other grassy slopes and open heaths. Range extends throughout Europe except for northern Britain and northern Scandinavia (where similar and closely related Northern Brown replaces it). Tends to be local; not rare. Easily confused with female Blues; submarginal band of prominent orange crescent marks, particularly strong in Spanish specimens, helps to identify. Sexes similar; female has more rounded wings and often bolder markings. Two broods, flying May–August. Principal foodplants rock rose on chalk and limestone, *Geranium* species on sand and clay. The larva hibernates.

Northern Brown Argus *Aricia artaxerxes* 25mm. Also known as the Mountain Argus. Occurs at high level in northern Britain (including Scotland), throughout most of Scandinavia, the Alps, Balkans and northern and central Spain. Local, seldom common. In Britain, distinguished from Brown Argus by white discoidal spot on forewing. In continental Europe identification is more difficult but forewing tends to have little or no orange submarginal band. There is a single brood; flies June and July. Larva feeds principally on rock rose and hibernates.

Mazarine Blue *Cyaniris seimargus* 30mm. Likes long grass, flowery meadows, hayfields and open countryside. Occurs from sea level to over 1,800m. Extinct in Britain but occurs almost universally elsewhere in Europe. Very widespread and can be common in suitable areas. Male violet-blue; female almost black. Underside, marked with white-edged black spots on mid-grey ground, has characters in common with that of Large Blue, but the Mazarine is smaller. Single brood; flies in June and July. The larva feeds on trefoils, sainfoin and related small Papilionaceae; hibernates.

Damon Blue *Agrodiaetus damon* 33mm. Mainly a mountain butterfly, frequenting hay meadows and open countryside with long grasses. Occurs in northern Spain and Pyrenees, Alps and eastwards into central Europe, north to Estonia and south to the Balkans; also found in central Italy. Local but often common in a restricted area. Male paler than many Blues; female dark brown. Both sexes have comet-like oblique streak across the underside hindwing which identifies the species, though this characteristic is found in a few rarer species of very limited range. Single brood, flying July–August. Larva feeds on sainfoin; hibernates when quite small.

Chapman's Blue *Agrodiaetus thersites* 32mm. Flies from low levels to mountains, frequenting grassy areas in the presence of the larval foodplant, sainfoin. Widespread in southern Europe; northern limits of range include northern Alps and Jura. Both sexes are very similar to the Common Blue, though the male is noticeably hairy and possibly more violet, and there is no underside spot in the forewing cell. There are two or more broods, flying from May–July, or longer. The larva hibernates.

Escher's Blue *Agrodiaetus escheri* 35–40mm. A south European species of hilly grassland and long grass meadows. Found in the eastern half of Spain, southern France, Italy and on the Baltic coast. Local, but not rare. Usually larger and brighter than the Common Blue but otherwise rather similar except for lack of underside spot in forewing cell. Female brown, with prominent inner marginal band of orange crescent marks. Single brood, flying in June and July. The larva feeds on milk vetch and sainfoin, and it hibernates.

Amanda's Blue *Agrodiaetus amanda* 40mm. Grassy banks and meadows are the habitat for this species, both lowland and in mountains. Several strongholds in eastern Spain, the range spreading eastwards along the French coast to the Alps, where it broadens north into Sweden, south to Italy and all regions to the east; absent from western France and Britain. Not rare. Soft texture and pale blue of the male help to identify. Larger than Turquoise Blue though upperside colouring somewhat similar. Single brood; flies June–July. The larva feeds on tufted vetch and sainfoin; hibernates.

Turquoise Blue *Plebicula dorylas* 32mm. A mountain butterfly found on grassy slopes. Common in some regions; usually at 1,000–2,000m. Rather scarce in northern Spain; the range extends through southern France, north into the Alps, central Europe and Poland; southern range includes Italy, the Balkans and Greece. Smaller than Amanda's Blue though the pale colour of the male is similar; the pale underside ground colour and prominent forewing black spotting help to identify. Sometimes two broods, flying May– July. The larva feeds on trefoils and other small Papilionaceae, also on thyme. Said to hibernate amongst dead florets.

Meleager's Blue *Meleageria daphnis* 40mm. Found in grassy hillsides, from low level to some altitude in mountains. A southern European butterfly, ranging from north-east Spain along southern France, Italy and then into central Europe, the Balkans and Greece. Common in places. Distinguished by the scalloped hindwings, visible in the male but prominent in the female. Both sexes are pale sky-blue but female forewing has dark fore-edge band and broad dark margins. Single brood, flying in June and July. The larva feeds on legumes and wild thyme; overwinters.

Chalkhill Blue *Lysandra coridon* 40mm. Flies almost exclusively on chalk and limestone, in open country, often on short turf interspersed with flowers. Occurs in central and northern Spain and otherwise throughout Europe, including southern Britain; absent from most of Scandinavia. Several geographical forms. Somewhat resembles the Provence Chalkhill Blue. There is a single brood, flying from June (July in the north) to August, between the two broods of the Provence species where this occurs. Larval foodplants are horseshoe vetch and allied vetches. Larva stays in the egg, fully formed, over winter.

Adonis Blue *Lysandra bellargus* 32mm. In Britain very local and becoming rarer; confined to small areas of downland. More widespread elsewhere in Europe on chalk grassland but still local. Occurs throughout the Continent, except for northern Britain and northern Scandinavia. Male colouring vivid iridescent blue, brighter than most other Blues; black-spotted white fringe distinguishes it from the Common Blue. Female usually brown but often with varying amounts of blue. Two broods which hardly overlap; flies May–June and July–August. The larva feeds on horseshoe vetch and hibernates.

Common Blue *Polyommatus icarus* 32mm. Flies in open spaces and grassland at almost all levels; may even stray into parks and gardens, especially in hot years. Widespread and common throughout the entire continent of Europe. Male blue, though colour variable and differences are seen between fresh and worn specimens. Female brown, usually with greater or lesser amounts of blue. Underside forewing cell contains spot, an important aid to identification. Successive broods; according to latitude, flight season may start as early as April and last into October. Larva feeds on clover, trefoils and many related plants; hibernates.

Grizzled Skipper *Pyrgus malvae* 20mm. Flies in open country, on grassy banks, and at edges of woodland, from low levels up to 1,800m. Occurs throughout Europe except northern Britain and northern Scandinavia. Common, though not seen in large numbers at a time. Sexes similar, male with more angular wings. One of many Skippers with similar markings but smaller than most and with more white markings, especially on hindwing, than others of its size. Rests with wings outspread. Two broods, except at high altitudes, flying April–August. Larval foodplants rock rose, wild strawberry and cinquefoil. Winter pupa.

Large Grizzled Skipper *Pyrgus alveus* 30mm. Found on grassland, especially in mountains where it is often common. Absent from Britain and northern Scandinavia but found otherwise throughout Europe. Underside white band very distinct but confusion with other species in this large and variable group of Skippers is difficult to avoid. One extended brood; flies June–August. Larval foodplants are rock rose, wild strawberry, cinquefoil and bramble. Hibernation is in the larval stage, except in Scandinavia, where the egg overwinters.

Dingy Skipper *Erynnis tages* 25mm. Often common on grassy slopes, in open country and rough, scrubby places. Found throughout Europe, including Britain, but absent from northern Scandinavia. Not as speckled as the Grizzled Skippers. Male has a scent-scale pouch on the leading edge of the forewing, and more angular wings. The resting position can be with wings outspread or as a moth with the wings closed, tent-like, over the body. Two broods; flies May–August. Larval foodplants are bird's foot trefoil, vetches and sea holly. The fully-grown larva spends the winter in a concealed hibernaculum.

Large Chequered Skipper *Heteropterus morpheus* 30mm. Lowland species only; inhabits light woodland and shaded grassy scrub. Range includes western France, northern areas of Spain, Italy and Germany, and much of eastern Europe from Lithuania in the north, down to the eastern Balkans. Very local and in widely scattered colonies. Sexes similar but female has more pronounced yellow markings on forewing and chequered fringes. Not confusable with other species and larger than all other Skippers. Single brood, flying in June and July. The larva feeds on grasses and reeds, usually in damp places, and here it hibernates.

Chequered Skipper
Caterocephalus palaemon 25mm. Flies in light woodland, rides and clearings, from sea level to over 1,000m in the Alps. Range includes most of France and central Europe, also most of northern Scandinavia; absent from most of Spain, Italy, central Scandinavia. In Britain, recently extinct in England but strong colonies exist in western Scotland. Rather local. The butterflies especially favour bugle flowers. Sexes similar but female has more rounded wings and larger, more open markings. Single brood, flies May and June. The larva feeds on grasses and hibernates.

Lulworth Skipper *Thymelicus acteon* 25mm. Flies on slopes of long grass, cliff tops and mountainsides. Range covers much of Europe, up to and including southern Britain (mainly on Dorset coast); absent from north-east Europe and Scandinavia. May be locally common. Sexes dissimilar; markings and ground colour variable in both. Female larger with a ring of pale orange spots, like a paw-print, on forewing. Male usually khaki, with oblique scent brand on forewing which shows less than in other species. Single brood, flies May–July. Larval foodplants are grasses. Young larva constructs a hibernaculum for the winter.

Essex Skipper *Thymelicus lineola* 25mm. Flies usually in long grasses, visiting flowers such as marjoram and rock rose, often on hillsides and in mountains. Range covers all of Europe except northern Britain and northern Scandinavia. Common in places. Almost indistinguishable from Small Skipper except for black spots on underside of antennae. Male distinguished by oblique sex brand, but often not distinct. Single brood, flying from May–August. Eggs are laid in the sheath of a grass stem where they remain unhatched for the winter. The larva feeds on grasses.

Small Skipper *Thymelicus sylvestris* 25mm. Very common in most grassy areas, from sea level to some 2,000m. Distributed throughout Europe except most of Scandinavia and the north of England. The male sex brand is usually more prominent than that of the Essex Skipper. The two species often fly together but the Small Skipper is usually the most abundant. The butterflies are particularly attracted to thistle, knapweed and burdock. There is one brood, flying from May–September. The larva feeds usually on soft grasses and passes the winter in the first instar.

Silver-spotted Skipper *Hesperia comma* 25mm. Found in grassland on chalk and limestone. In southern Britain only a few colonies, favouring short-cropped turf and flying in August. Elsewhere in Europe found in long grass, July–August. Range includes all of Europe except northern Britain and northern Scandinavia. Usually very local. Can be confused with Large Skipper but underside white spotting on green separates them; upperside darker and less orange; pale yellow spotting more prominent. Male has oblique dark sex brand on forewing; female has pale yellow spotting on both forewing and hindwing. Larval foodplants are grasses. Winter egg.

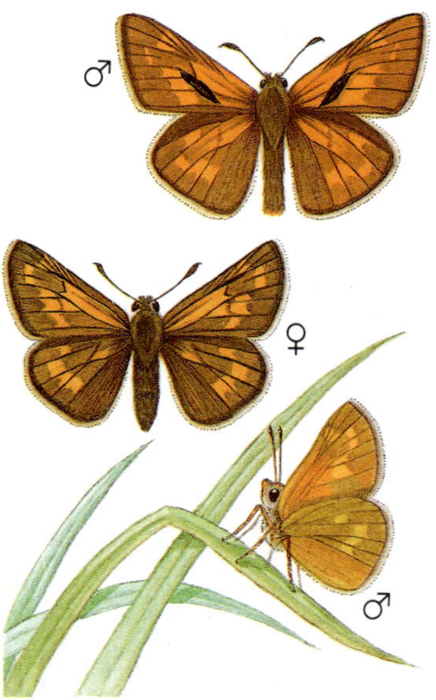

Large Skipper *Ochlodes venata* 25mm. Very common in most kinds of grassland and at all levels up to 2,000m. Distributed throughout Europe except south coast of Spain and northern Scandinavia. More orange than Silver-spotted Skipper and underside spotting is not as white. In male oblique sex brand on forewing is very prominent; female has brighter spotting on forewing and hindwing. In northern regions there is one brood in June and July but further south there may be two or more broods over several months. The larva feeds on grasses and hibernates when partially grown.

Field Notes

Further Reading

Carter, D. and Hargreaves, B., *Field Guide to Caterpillars in Britain and Europe*. Collins, London, 1986.
Specialises in the larvae of Lepidoptera.

Chinery, M. (Ed.), *New Generation Guide: Butterflies and Day-flying Moths of Britain and Europe*. Collins, London, 1989.
Covers many aspects of the biology, evolution and ecology of Lepidoptera.

Goodden, R., *British Butterflies: A Field Guide*. David & Charles, Newton Abbot, 1978.
Describes habitat, life history, distribution and habits.

Higgins, L. and Hargreaves, B., *Field Guide to Butterflies of Britain and Europe*. Collins, London, 1983.
Comprehensive guide to all European species.

Thomas, J., *Guide to Butterflies of the British Isles*. Royal Society for Nature Conservation, Lincoln, 1986.
Describes habitat, life history, distribution and habits.

Thomas, J. and Lewington, R., *Butterflies of Britain and Ireland*. Dorling Kindersley, London 1991.
Covers all British species.

Whalley, P., *Pocket Guide to Butterflies*. Mitchell Beazley, London, 1981.
Covers all European species.

Useful Addresses

Amateur Entomologist's Society
22 Salisbury Road, Feltham, Middx TW13 5DP.
Encourages amateur interest in entomology. Ideal for the young as well as the experienced.

British Entomological and Natural History Society
74 South Audley Street, London W1Y 5FF.
National society, mainly for the more experienced entomologist.

Butterfly Conservation
PO Box 22, Dedham, Essex CO7 6EY.
Twenty-five local branches across the country. The principal butterfly conservation organisation.

Countryside Council for Wales
Ladywell House, Newtown, Powys SY16 1RD.

English Nature
Northminster House, Peterborough PE1 1UA.

Nature Conservancy Council for Scotland
12 Hope Terrace, Edinburgh EH9 2AS.

Royal Entomological Society of London
41 Queen's Gate, London SW7 5HR.
National society for the experienced and professional entomologist.

Royal Society for Nature Conservation
The Green, Witham Park, Waterside South, Lincoln LN5 7JR.
The parent body of the county Trusts for Nature Conservation.

Index

Index

Index